Notes & Apologies:

★ This issue of *The Believer* is dedicated to Tom Luddy, the ultimate believer in *The Believer*. When we published our first issue of the magazine in 2003, Tom Luddy was a stalwart supporter, and with his boundless enthusiasm, and gift for connecting people, he introduced us to countless interview subjects and writers. It was Tom who had faith in our magazine at the start, especially at times when we did not. This world lost Tom Luddy on February 13, 2023. He will be forever missed.

★ Rejoice! Our podcast, *Constellation Prize*, is back. In this four-part miniseries, host Bianca Giaever and poet Terry Tempest Williams embark on a shared artistic and spiritual quest. The plan is to take long nightwalks—Terry in Utah and Bianca in Vermont—in the hopes of encountering God. Bianca's grandfather thinks the project is dumb. Bianca has her own doubts. But Terry feels confident they will succeed, and maybe she's right. Listen wherever podcasts are available and then tell all your friends to listen too.

★ On page 86, you'll find an eight-page excerpt from *Are You Willing to Die for the Cause? Revolution in 1960s Quebec* by Chris Oliveros. Oliveros's book is a deeply researched history of the FLQ (Front de libération du Québec, or the Quebec Liberation Front), a violent revolutionary movement that, over the course of seven years, initiated a series of attempts to overthrow the Canadian government. The book is forthcoming in October of this year from Drawn & Quarterly.

★ The incidental illustrations in this issue are by Niv Bavarsky.

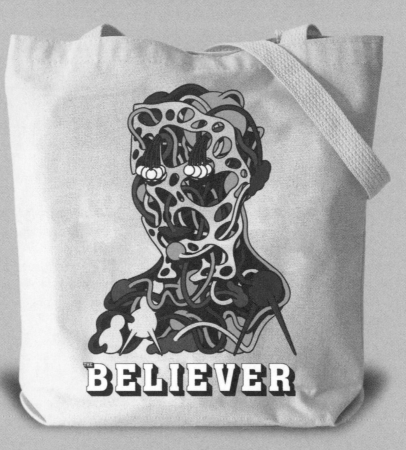

# DEAR THE BELIEVER

849 VALENCIA STREET, SAN FRANCISCO, CA 94110

*letters@thebeliever.net*

**Dear Believer,**

I enjoyed Michael Imperioli's musings on *Goodfellas* (Spring 2023) and the unfortunate fate of Billy Batts. When he described the film's opening as "very 'Mack the Knife,'" I went down a bit of a wormhole of "Mack the Knife" recordings. There's the Louis Armstrong recording, the Ella Fitzgerald version, the hoarse recording by Dave Van Ronk, and the popular Bobby Darin rendition, to name a few. The list of people who have recorded it is just astonishing. I think the Ella Fitzgerald one is probably the best. Just my opinion. One thing I learned during my Mack studies is that the song was actually a last-minute addition to the original play [*The Threepenny Opera*], because the actor who played Macheath thought his character needed a better introduction.

Anyway, this concludes my commentary on "Mack the Knife." Thank you for listening.

*John Stein*
*New York, NY*

**Dear Believer,**

I thought Andrea Bajani's story in issue 141 ("The Curse of Kafka," Spring 2023) was brilliant. What a fascinating writer. I loved the resonance between transplants and fiction. He captured both subjects with such delicacy, and I kept finding myself surprised by the turns that the essay took. There was also just a powerful honesty undergirding all of it. I think the last lines of the piece will stay with me for some time. Glad he didn't actually quit writing.

*Aaron Brooks*
*Memphis, TN*

**Dear Believer,**

I was pleased to read Nick Hornby's postulation that men are perhaps finished as an authorial class. I agree.

Sincerely,
*Dolores*
*USA*

**Dear Believer,**

While I mostly found it fascinating, I have to tell you that Ginger Greene's schema ("Paint by Numbers," Spring 2023) sort of stressed me out. As an artist, something about seeing the category "output rate per working year" was just too overwhelming. It was sort of like looking at that data visualization of how many days you likely have left in your life. I can't remember who made that, but obviously it sort of puts it all in perspective, the scarcity of time, the urgency. I'm not stoned right now, if that's what you're wondering. I'm just a girl who recently saw the lifetime output of major artists and is reckoning with her own mortality. Quantity isn't quality obviously, but you do need *some* quantity. Back to work, I guess. Thanks for freaking me out,

*Jenny Smith*
*Los Angeles, CA*

**Dear Believer,**

I know you're not going to publish this, but I'm going to write it anyway. I've written you many letters and you never publish them. You likely won't publish [end of letter]

*Unsigned*

**Dear Believer,**

I had no idea how much I'd missed the real you until you returned.

Welcome back.
*Doron Klemer*
*New Orleans, LA*

**Dear Believer,**

I loved the description of Alan Alda's meet-cute (Winter 2022/2023). I thought I'd write to share the story of my own. I'm now eighty-one and my husband is seventy-nine. One day, when I was in my twenties, I went horsebacking with a friend outside of Boston. People used to do that, ride horses near Boston. Anyway, I wasn't good at horseback riding, and my horse bucked me to the ground. I was pretty shaken up, and didn't want to get back on the horse, but my friend told me she had a friend nearby, who could help us. So we walked—I don't know how I walked but I did—a mile to her friend's house. He took me in and set me up in a guest bedroom to recover. I thought, Who is this cute man who has saved me? The rest was history.

*Marianne Thomas*
*Palm Beach, FL*

CAN
PLEASURE
ALSO BE
POLITICAL?

P. 81

I SLEEP AND
THEN I WAKE
UP SORT OF
VIBRATING.

*p. 55*

*Compiled by Emily Lang; Portraits by Kristian Hammerstad*

THERE IS NO GREAT
PROGRAMMER
DICTATING WHAT I SEE. *p. 16*

I DON'T HAVE
NEURONS?
OK, WHAT
THE HELL
AM I? *p. 40*

# UNDERWAY

WE ASK WRITERS AND ARTISTS: WHAT'S ON YOUR DESK? WHAT ARE YOU WORKING ON?

*by Morgan Talty*

**Tell Me Your Life Story, Dad**

*Even though she never finished it, my mom wrote one of these for me, and since her death, in February 2021, it's one of my most cherished belongings. I want my son, Charlie, to have one too.*

**Seashell**

*This is one of my mother's keepsakes. She had tons of them (a heart-shaped rock, for example). I like that when I put this shell to my ear, I can still hear the sound of her voice saying, "Morgan, can you get me a pack of smokes?"*

**Pencil-and-Pen Organizer**

*It's just for looks and makes me feel like I have my life together. But every now and then I need a pen or a pencil or a paper clip.*

**Vape**

*I quit smoking about seven years ago and switched to vaping. Now that I have a son, I don't vape inside, so this is just an empty one I use to hold when I'm taking a break from writing and need to think.*

**Basket**

*This was gifted to me and my wife, Jorden, from my mother. I don't think she had room for it or wanted to deal with it, so she gave it to us. Now I'm stuck with it.*

**Glass Vase Filled with Feathers**

*My mother was an avid feather collector. She would spend hours outside looking for them. These are just a few of the feathers she collected and put in a vase. However, one of the feathers was gifted to me by a fellow Indigenous person after a book event for* Night of the Living Rez.

**Sweetgrass**

*The smell reminds me of so many memories, and when I write, the best way for me to conjure emotion is to remember.*

**Planner**

*I literally would not know what to do if I didn't have one.*

Currently I'm wrapping up edits to my debut novel, *Fire, Exit*, which will be out from Tin House in summer 2024. The novel uses blood quantum—a colonial tool that further enacts Indigenous erasure—to propel a narrative in which a woman lies about who her daughter's father is so she can be an enrolled member of the tribe. The story is told from the point of view of the real father, a non-native, who is trying to reconnect with his dying mother while building the courage to tell his daughter the truth. I'm also at work on another project, a book of memoir, that looks at my family and tries to make sense of my mother's and father's deaths. This would explain why so many things on my desk are related to my mom—I've been writing a great deal about her. In a way, I like to think that this book—however it will end up—will one day show my son the grandparents he never met. ✶

*Illustration by Kristian Hammerstad*

# ASK CARRIE

A QUARTERLY COLUMN FROM
CARRIE BROWNSTEIN, WHO IS BETTER
AT DISPENSING ADVICE THAN TAKING IT

*Send questions to advice@thebeliever.net*

---

**Q:** *This past year, I developed a crush on a guy who works in the same building as me. Although we talk nearly every day, it took me over five months to ask him for his phone number. Since then, we have been texting sporadically. Sometimes it takes him one or two days to respond, but more recently, it has taken him a little over a week to respond to one of my texts. While I don't want to appear too desperate, I usually respond to his texts right away (or within a day or so at most). All my friends say he is not worth it and that I should move on. What do you think? Should I give up on this chance for love? Or should I outwardly declare my feelings to him?*

*Hopelessly in Love, Hartford, CT*

---

 A few years ago I found myself in a similar predicament. Tell me if this sounds familiar: You send a text, one carefully crafted to hit that sweet spot of witty but not silly, smart but not supercilious, sincere but not overly earnest, flirty but not desperate. There's a lot to balance, which is why you've previewed your text in the Notes app. You hit SEND. Then for a few seconds—a whole minute, if you're lucky—you feel a sense of calm. The serenity, unfortunately, is fleeting. Because now your entire life—okay, not your *life* per se, just your mood, appetite, attention span, sleep patterns, energy, and will to go on—is dependent on the reply. When the response doesn't arrive within an appropriate time frame (immediately would be preferable, but who's keeping track?!), you resort to magical thinking. When I was in the throes of this dynamic and didn't receive a reply within a few hours, I literally thought, She probably died. *Death!* That is where my brain went, as opposed to the dozens of logical reasons for her lack of engagement, starting with the most obvious one: my feelings were unrequited. Worse, of course, is when you finally receive a text back: the internal debate as to how long you should wait to respond is excruciating—embarrassing, really. I probably spent more time on that mental equation than I ever did on high school algebra. So I really do have sympathy for you. But this is a terrible dynamic, anxiety-producing and enervating. Your friends are right: it's not worth it. A better use of your energy would be to extricate yourself from this text message purgatory and focus on people who make you feel valued, secure, and loved. It's so cliché, but I promise that if the crush is mutual, this guy will let you know.

---

**Q:** *My identical twin sister recently got married. However, despite this, her husband on occasion* still *mixes us up, which really bothers her. Most of the time he gets it*

*Illustration by Kristian Hammerstad*

*right, but every once in a while he messes up. Is this a red flag to you? Many other people in our lives seem to be able to tell us apart with ease.*

    *Clarissa*
    *San Francisco, CA*

**A:** Is it a red flag to me? I need some context. A quiz: If he had two golden retrievers with blond flowing hair, would he need to put a bandanna on one of them? If his black Audi Q5 was parked next to another black Audi Q5, would he reach for the wrong door handle? Is he a man who mixes up the capitals of North and South Carolina? Are the words *there*, *their*, and *they're* interchangeable for him? I want to make sure your brother-in-law isn't a guy who is *known* for his confusion about similar-sounding and -looking people and things. If he isn't, then I think there's something further to explore. I'd start by suggesting that your sister tell her husband that his identity mix-ups hurt her feelings. Perhaps her honesty will elicit some self-reflection on his part, such as *What is keeping me from truly seeing my wife?*; *Am I afraid of emotional intimacy?*; and *Should I have married a fraternal twin instead?* Giving your sister's husband the benefit of the doubt, I'm guessing that once he knows that the mix-ups bother his wife, he'll be more careful and attentive. Ultimately, your sister wants reassurance that when it comes to the man she's married, there's no confusing her for anyone else, even her own twin sister. So I hope your brother-in-law can understand how for your sister, his occasional errors are not merely about mistaken identity but about her need to feel like a unique person.

---

## FICTIONAL UNIVERSITIES IN NOVELS

* ✶ College-on-the-Hill (*White Noise*, Don DeLillo)
* ✶ Waindell College (*Pnin*, Vladimir Nabokov)
* ✶ Mentor University (*Been Down So Long It Looks Like Up to Me*, Richard Fariña)
* ✶ Hampden College (*The Secret History,* Donna Tartt)
* ✶ Jack London College (*Japanese by Spring*, Ishmael Reed)
* ✶ Athena College (*The Human Stain*, Philip Roth)
* ✶ Wellington College (*On Beauty*, Zadie Smith)
* ✶ Corbin University (*The Netanyahus*, Joshua Cohen)
* ✶ Dupont University (*I Am Charlotte Simmons*, Tom Wolfe)
* ✶ New Tammany College (*Giles Goat-Boy*, John Barth)
* ✶ Corinth University (*The War Between the Tates*, Alison Lurie)
* ✶ University of Rummidge (*Small World*, David Lodge)
* ✶ Camden College (*The Rules of Attraction*, Bret Easton Ellis)
* ✶ Beauchamp University (*As She Climbed Across the Table*, Jonathan Lethem)
* ✶ Cape Technical University (*Disgrace*, J. M. Coetzee)
* ✶ Carlyle University (*The Matlock Paper*, Robert Ludlum)
* ✶ Centauri University (*Empire Star*, Samuel R. Delany)
* ✶ Watson-Crick Institute (*Oryx and Crake*, Margaret Atwood)
* ✶ University of Mars (*Icehenge*, Kim Stanley Robinson)
* ✶ Blackstock College (*Tam Lin*, Pamela Dean)

    —*list compiled by Katherine Williams*

**Q:** *I've always been picky about the kinds of TV shows and films I watch. If I'm going to sink hours of my time into watching something, I want it to be worth it. Recently, I haven't found any show or film that holds my attention. My friends constantly recommend popular TV shows or films they've enjoyed. Occasionally, I start the first episode of a show or ten minutes of a film, but I can't get into it. I don't even know what I want to watch anymore, and I can't rewatch things. I think my friends are also getting tired of me complaining about wasting more of my time looking for something to watch than actually watching anything. What should I do?*

    *Sincerely,*
    *Margaret Clayton*
    *Atlanta, GA*

**A:** Assuming your friends have taste, and knowing you've rejected their recommendations, I fear my own suggestions will be in vain. Which is why I think you should give up on TV and films altogether. Your friends will be as annoyed by your new proclamation as they were by your complaints that there's nothing to watch. But now they'll feel judged, which means they'll be forced to defend their habits. These justifications will be complex, heartwarming, and maybe even thrilling. From comedy to drama, absurd to experimental, you'll witness a plethora of genres. Margaret, your friends' passionate explanations about why they watch TV and films—and why you shouldn't give up on these mediums—will be event viewing. Grab your popcorn.

---

**Q:** *I've been a copywriter for over thirty years, and I seem to have found myself in danger of being replaced by a machine. My bosses were whispering about salaries and layoffs the other day, and I've been freaking out ever since. Are you worried about AI taking over human jobs? Do you think I'm being paranoid?*
*Sincerely,*
*Jean*
*New York, NY*

**A:** I forwarded your question to an AI language model. It told me that the idea of AI taking over human jobs was a "complex and ongoing discussion… It is unlikely that it will completely replace most human jobs." I don't know about you, but I don't feel reassured. An ongoing discussion between whom? Sure, we know it's a human debate, but are the robots also meeting on this? And what do they mean by "unlikely"? That's a word sorely lacking in specificity.

Wouldn't AI, with all its algorithmic and predictive abilities, be able to give us some data, some numbers? Is it lying? Can it lie? Wait: I'll ask. It told me, "I don't have intentions, desires, or emotions, so I am not capable of lying in the same way that a human being might be." Whew. Glad AI's not going to deceive us in some boring humanistic way. Then I asked it why humans fear AI, and it answered that we fear the unknown. OK: trite but valid. It added that humans are scared that AI "could be used for malicious purposes," and, whoa, it's also blaming our perceptions on "popular culture depictions of rogue or malevolent AI, such as *The Terminator* or *The Matrix*." I guess even AI is concerned about representation. The last inquiry I posed to my AI interlocutor was whether it would be a good advice columnist. While it noted that it would certainly "provide objective and data-driven insights not influenced by personal bias or subjective opinions," it also said that most people would prefer advice from a human's more "empathetic approach." So, Jean, that is what I offer you: my empathy. Despite the uncertainty you face, try not to be paranoid. Try instead to remember you have a heart; you have feelings and experiences and a point of view. Not everything can be replaced or replicated. ✶

---

## GOYA PAINTINGS FEATURING A SMALL DOG

✶ *The Dog*, 1819–23
✶ *Dogs on a Leash*, 1775
✶ *The White Duchess*, 1795
✶ *Portrait of Joaquina Candado Ricarte*, 1802
✶ *Doña Francisca Vicenta Chollet and Gentleman*, 1806
✶ *Charles III in Hunting Costume*, 1787
✶ *The Swing*, 1779
✶ *The Snowstorm or Winter*, 1786
✶ *Hunting Party*, 1775
✶ *Picnic on the Banks of the Manzanares*, 1776
✶ *A Fight at the Venta Nueva*, 1777
✶ *The Parasol*, 1777
✶ *The Kite*, 1777–78
✶ *The Pottery Vendor*, 1779
✶ *Portrait of María Teresa de Borbón y Vallabriga*, 1783
✶ *The School Scene*, 1785
✶ *Marquesa Mariana de Pontejos*, 1786
✶ *King Charles IV in Hunting Costume*, 1799

—*list compiled by Katherine Williams*

# RESURRECTOR

A ROTATING GUEST COLUMN IN WHICH WRITERS REEXAMINE CRITICALLY UNACCLAIMED WORKS OF ART. IN THIS ISSUE: *THE DECLINE OF WESTERN CIVILIZATION, PART II: THE METAL YEARS*

*by John Wray*

Hidden halfway through *The Decline of Western Civilization, Part II: The Metal Years*, Penelope Spheeris's love-it-or-loathe-it documentary about '80s glam metal, is a modest little scene that freed my teenage brain from decades of cultural indoctrination. I'm referring, of course, to the infamous Dude-in-the-Pool interview, featuring W.A.S.P. guitarist Chris Holmes, three bottles of Smirnoff, an inflatable pool recliner, and his mom.

In the scene, a handsome blond man is floating on his back in the pool of a Hollywood mansion, telling us he's dreamed of being a rock star ever since he was a child. In spite of his grin, we know something is seriously wrong. Maybe the grin itself is the tip-off—that, or the look on the face of his mother, hunched and silent in a deck chair a few feet away. Immediately after telling Spheeris that he has "five, six, ten, twelve" gold records, Holmes pours the better part of a fifth of vodka down his throat and calls himself a "piece of crap" and a "full-blown alcoholic"—as if we need to be enlightened on that score. "I don't dig the person I am," he mumbles, almost apologetically, and for an instant we glimpse the polite and bashful boy he must have been. He offers his mother a drink, lets out a cackle of unadulterated suffering, and announces, with a toothy all-American smile: "I'm a happy camper." Then he lets himself disappear into the pool.

I was twenty years old when I first saw that footage of Holmes. I have very little insight into the soul of the greasy-haired meathead I was at that age, but I must still have been in thrall to the elemental myth of the entertainment industry—*talent equals fame equals wealth equals happiness equals self-respect*—because those four and a half minutes shocked me. The presence of Holmes's mother is a significant part of what makes the Dude-in-the-Pool interview so haunting—a feature-length doc about their dynamic would have given *Grey Gardens* a run for its money. I laughed out loud, I remember—the film can be side-splittingly funny—but years later, that scene was still alive and twitching in my brain.

None of which is to say that *DWCII* isn't as joyously sleazy as the viewer might hope and expect. Among its darkly glittering delights are Kiss's Paul Stanley soliloquizing about group sex from a satin-sheeted waterbed, surrounded by lingerie-clad women; Megadeth's Dave Mustaine explaining why beer is the omphalos of his personal cosmology; and Ozzy Osbourne, in what looks disturbingly like a Tipper Gore hairpiece, holding forth on the dangers of drug abuse while frying eggs and bacon in a pan. Spheeris's film was condescended to by the mainstream media when it premiered, and it's not hard to understand why; I remember feeling no small amount of embarrassment myself, after that momentous first viewing, by how much I adored it. The year before last, however, while researching a book about metal, I watched *DWCII* again—and finally recognized it as a frost-tipped masterpiece.

The simple passage of time has rendered its subject matter more profound—the starry-eyed goofballs that Spheeris raps with about their plans for global domination seem less ridiculous than tragic. What's most mesmerizing to me now are the rapid-fire interviews with total unknowns: the Strip Rats and Strip Kittens, the Chris Holmes wannabes, each of them on-screen for just a few seconds. The experience of flitting from one lost cause to the next is both punishing and bewitching. They're all utterly certain they're going to be megastars, reflexively parroting the great rock platitudes. I could quote a dozen lines from memory:

> I wouldn't mind being a rock star... as long as "rock star" is defined as rich... and rich.
> I think it will come pretty easily to me—because I'm, you know, different from everyone else.
> When you doubt it is when you lose it, man.

They're all such happy campers. ✷

*Illustration by Madison Ketcham*

# THE PROCESS
## IN WHICH AN ARTIST DISCUSSES MAKING A PARTICULAR WORK
Patrick Martinez, *Promised Land*, 2022

Walking down any concrete artery in Los Angeles, you may pass some of the elements and ideas in Patrick Martinez's grand 7' × 16' abstracted landscape painting, Promised Land. A Pasadena and San Gabriel native, Martinez creates layered work that reflects his connection to the region and to the graffiti he grew up writing in the early '90s with his crew, HDS (Hitting Dope Spots). As a teenager, he submitted his black book—a graffiti writer's sketchbook that includes inscriptions and drawings— as a portfolio to the Visual Arts and Design Academy, a specialized art high school. At VADA, he met and became inspired by teacher and artist Mark Ayala. Like Ayala, Martinez went on to earn a degree from ArtCenter College of Design, which he graduated from in 2005 with a BFA.

Promised Land, *like much of Martinez's work, responds to his life in the city and its surroundings, and the disenfranchisement of people of color. It features images of pre-Columbian Cacaxtla battle warriors and painted palm trees, and incorporates other, more physical elements, like a fallen vinyl banner, geometric tiles, and neon signage. Through this mixture of materials, Martinez evokes a cultural environment that is constantly being destroyed, rebuilt, and gentrified. I spoke to him about the work at Charlie James Gallery in Los Angeles's Chinatown.*
—Trina Calderón

*Acrylic, stucco, neon, Mean Streak, ceramic, spray paint, latex house paint, banner tarp, ceramic tile, tile adhesive, family-archive photo collage on panel. 84 × 192 × 7 in. Courtesy of the artist.*

THE BELIEVER: How did you begin to imagine this painting?

PATRICK MARTINEZ: My first entry point to painting was graffiti. I understood that the city was like an addition-subtraction game. My friends and me, we started adding to the city, and then the city would take things out. Or people that owned the shop, or whatever you wrote on, would take away what you did. It was this community game of tag. I was always interested in that, and the way things are changing.

I understand in my head what I'm trying to say with a piece. A lot of the ideas that come into my mind these days are about land—especially now, when I have a child, and I want to own a piece of it. A lot of people in Los Angeles just want to occupy space in the city they grew up in. When I started thinking about the piece, I started thinking about that.

My approach is pretty traditional. If you really peel back the layers, I deal with landscapes, figures, portraits, and that's pretty much it. In the tradition of art history, I feel like that's traditional, but I try to turn all that stuff on its head.

In approaching this landscape, I did some things in a traditional way. When I started it, I knew I was going to start with Central Mexican murals, brown bodies that you might see at community centers, parks, middle schools, elementary schools. Painted on stuccos and handball courts. I imagined that kind of mural on stucco, so I started with stucco, brown, and primer, white. Then I started painting on top of it with Cacaxtla battle murals.

BLVR: What does it mean to have the pre-Columbian figures as your background?

PM: I think about them as brown bodies. In the Americas, brown bodies were here first. Layering them and showing the layers on top of them are the language of my ideas, and are all signifiers of years of that talk of wanting people to "go back to where they came from." We've been here. Before anything, there were brown folks walking around.

BLVR: How did you come up with the title?

PM: In Los Angeles, when I'm making work, I almost think about it as though I'm making a postcard of the place. It's beautiful, but it's tough out here. People really struggle to figure things out. There's financial violence going on. There are things that you used to be able to afford that you can't afford. It's this subtle kind of slipping away of things.

I thought about that when I started making the piece; I thought about it when I was close to finishing it and titling it. It's a weird thing, because I have family that has moved away and has been priced out of Los Angeles. So it's like this postcard saying, *Oh, it's so beautiful here. Who wants to come?* But also, not really.

BLVR: It's a facade.

PM: It's a facade, and then something is built on top of that facade. I'm layering murals on top of one another, washing them out, tagging on them.

BLVR: I feel like these colors speak to California. They speak to old graffiti too. What do they mean in this work?

PM: I think about that, why I come back to certain colors. Often, when I see something in the city, I sample it. I try to figure out a way to use it in the paintings. Pink is something that comes up in a lot of the graffiti I've done. Also, the colors of storefronts that are dilapidated. They're still kind of standing, like barbershops and things on Whittier Boulevard. It's not part of this aesthetic that has been dictated to us via new high-rises and what's supposed to be valuable. It's almost like the opposite of what "sleek" is supposed to look like in Los Angeles. I'm looking at all that and I'm wanting to do the opposite and celebrate the discounted and the overlooked.

BLVR: You've used many materials in this artwork before: stucco, tiles, ceramic, neon. What's the process like in terms of layering them?

PM: I start by organizing materials by the size I want. I do it from left to right. I throw materials on there and try to equalize them, even them out. Even though it's chaotic, I'm figuring out what I'm trying to say with the materials, and what the materials can add.

Then I start going for it on the panel. There are points where I just get stuck and I'm like, This piece, the idea was this, and it's not reading like that right now. At one point, with this piece, I was driving home and I saw this tarp, right there in Vernon. I was like: That's kind of the rhythm that I need in the piece. Just things like that—the land provides. If you're paying attention, it'll show you, like, *Oh, yeah. Oh, you need it? OK. Here you go.*

BLVR: In this layering process, at what point do you know: I need light. Or: I'm going to bring in neon?

PM: It's in the middle of it. If I'm doing a stucco piece, it always comes up because I always think about storefronts and how they're designed. I'm trying to celebrate that and inject that into the piece somehow. The neon palm trees: they work as something that you might find in a storefront.

BLVR: And what about the photographs set inside the neon signage?

PM: This is from my family archive, my mother's side and my father's side. My mom came from the Philippines in the '70s, and her family followed. My dad's family has been here for a long time. It's that crazy dynamic. I do these as kind of cyan prints of them to show time passing. It makes them look like a poster in a hair salon or barbershop—they're sun-kissed. To me that speaks to time, but also more specifically to LA weather.

BLVR: Using all these materials in a collage is an abstract way to meditate on that relationship with time within the landscape. How do the ceramic roses find their place in this narrative?

PM: The rose is something that I hand-make, each one of them, out of clay. The idea comes from street memorials. It's abstracted, because I'm sticking them to the surface of the stucco. But the street memorials, if you've ever seen them in any city, you see the combination of hard and soft roses. People leave this kind of thing wherever someone got hit by a car, or shot, or whatever. Someone lost a life. It's a memorial, kind of makeshift. That's part of the landscape, so I'm using that and abstracting it a little bit.

BLVR: What is the most challenging part for you in making this painting?

PM: The size of it. It was very physical. It was on the wall when I was making it, but really being able to physically put it together was the most challenging part. It's real labor: cutting tile, placing tile, painting layers and layers of paint with rollers.

BLVR: How did you know when you were finished?

PM: I knew I wanted the piece to almost feel like sound. Like when it gets too loud, the beat gets too loud, and it distorts, and it's almost kind of this shaking. It's interesting, because that's really what I think about when I start something. I want it to feel kind of like that.

My brother used to have a Toyota truck, and he used to have Cerwin Vega speakers in the back with a Rockford Fosgate amp. He used to bump loud. In the '90s we used to drive around, and he used to bump loud. I think about that a lot: Well, what do you want your work to do? I want it to bother people like that. I want it to bother people and the cars next to us. You know what I mean?

BLVR: Hell yeah.

PM: Just kind of like, *Fuck, what… what are you…?* I feel like my brother turned it up all the way because he felt it was the truth and he wanted people to hear it. ✫

---

### EXHAUSTIVE LIST OF THINGS SYLVIE FISHER HAS IN HER POCKETS IN MARILYNNE ROBINSON'S *HOUSEKEEPING*

✫ A little ball of paper money and some change
✫ Ruth's hand
✫ A cold hand
✫ Fisted hands
✫ Saltines
✫ A Mountain Bar
✫ Fish
✫ Crackers
✫ Gum wrappers
✫ Ticket stubs

*—list compiled by Emma-Li Downer*

# CLOSE READ

UNPACKING ONE REDOUBTABLE PASSAGE.

THIS ISSUE: *GHOSTS OF NEW YORK* BY JIM LEWIS

*by Benjamin Anastas*

*and his journalism. He lives in Austin, and the New York in* Ghosts *has the quality of a found Kodachrome print: saturated colors, a vanished world reclaimed.*

*Here is a short list of great New York City novels, in chronological order: Ann Petry's* The Street *(1946), Saul Bellow's* Seize the Day *(1956), Paula Fox's* Desperate Characters *(1970), Chang-rae Lee's* Native Speaker *(1995), Teju Cole's* Open City *(2011). Jim Lewis's* Ghosts of New York *belongs in this company: it's "a portrait in chemicals" of the city and its restless strivers.*

*Jim Lewis's novel* Ghosts of New York *came out on April Fools' Day, 2021, the same day the FDA approved the first at-home rapid antigen tests for COVID-19. There was a positive review on the* New York Times *website that day, calling* Ghosts *"a wondrous novel, with prose that sparkles like certain sidewalks after rain," followed by a couple of online events, and then* Ghosts of New York *pretty much vanished.*

*This scene would be too easy, too romantic, without this remnant of an act of violence. There is something tender underway, a love affair is starting, yet there is this mystery—the afterimage of a swinging baseball bat.*

*"Johnny and Bridget" is an eighty-seven-page novella that forms the novel's heart. It's about a love triangle between Mike, a graduate student at Columbia; Bridget, who is at Barnard; and Johnny, Mike's regal friend from an unnamed West African country. The dramatic setup is fairly traditional, but the story is not: it migrates through time and brings its characters into geopolitics and treats their fates like something written in the holy scripture of New York.*

*The novel is told in episodes: underneath the pavement of words is a subway system of connections, but every individual section stands on its own. Some are lyric meditations on the city's unknown dead, others are character portraits in prose, still others like the long shots of Manhattan streets in Chantal Akerman's* News from Home *(1976).*

*The simple past is used to quiet the city down: there are just Mike and Bridget doing a "stoop walk," that post-date ritual when all we know of the person we are walking with is the stoop of their building and the outside of their door. "I'm right here" is just the right line—as is the question "Where are you?"*

*This is pure F. Scott Fitzgerald—the lilt and desire, the excess and precision. The line keeps you a little off-balance: How can they be snowing? An indulgence, but it fits the moment in the story.*

*More F. Scott!*

*There are moments when the city stops. I'm thinking of blizzards, of 9/11, of early in the pandemic. Lovers can also stop the city when they are deep inside a "stoop walk." And the complications of their love affair are already present, in the pause before the city goes back to its great churning of lives.*

**W**e were about halfway up the block when she stopped and turned. I wasn't sure why. I'm right here, she said, pointing over her shoulder.

The building with the broken window in the doorway. Where are you?

We passed it a few blocks back, I said.

You're walking me to my door. I nodded and she hesitated, trying to decide whether that made me a good man or one on the make, and in any case what the difference was and which she preferred. She cocked her head and frowned. At the top of her stoop there was a metal door with a thick pane of reinforced glass, which nevertheless had a silvery crack running through it, glowing from the gun-blue light of the fluorescent bulb in the hallway behind. It must have taken considerable force to do that kind of damage, a baseball bat or a metal pipe; I was hoping it wasn't somebody's head. There was such mystery to violence, arising suddenly and then retreating again, leaving nothing behind but something broken, and no way of knowing how it happened, no one to ask. Bridget was silent, and I turned. She was looking at me but she didn't say anything.

We're snowing, I said.

She didn't move, but she winced slightly. Say that again.

We're snowing, you and me.

We stood there, the two of us, and looked at each other, without touching, without moving; it wasn't a stare-down, exactly, there was no aggression in it, but neither was it simply curiosity. It was a kind of mutual appeal, and it seemed to last a very long time, though it might have been just a second, or less than that—a brief hold placed on the winter city, the girl with the breath of a smile on her face. Then her smile broadened, and with dazzling purity she quickly rose up on her toes, kissed my cheek, then turned and walked up the half dozen stairs into the vestibule of her apartment building, fetching her keys from her bag and vanishing through the door, leaving me alone on the street, listening to the cold noises along the block. ★

*Illustrations by Annie Dills*

# HOW TO WALK AROUND NEW YORK

ACCOMPANYING DOCUMENTARY FILMMAKER JOHN WILSON AS HE SEARCHES FOR
DISCARDED BOTTLES OF URINE

*by Amy Fusselman*

### 1.

John Wilson's HBO docu-comedy series, *How To with John Wilson*, is multi-layered, to put it mildly. In the guise of an instructional video, the show combines hyper-curated scenes of only–in–New York City strangeness, Wilson's deftly edited interviews with everyday weirdos he doesn't name, and his uniquely staccato second-person narration, to create brilliant and funny visual essays that have earned him a devoted following and critical acclaim.

The show has aired for two seasons; its highly anticipated third and final season will premiere on July 28. Its writers' room boasts a startling array of talent: best-selling author Susan Orlean, Orlean's fellow *New Yorker* scribe Alice Gregory, *Nathan for You* alum Michael Koman, and the gloriously unhinged comedian Conner O'Malley.

Wilson is remarkably reticent as the host of his own TV show. He's almost never on camera, and when he is, it's only in footage from the past, or when his hand, or maybe his shoe, appears in the frame as he films. Despite this stance, he has managed to make some singularly personal work. Part of the attraction of the series is the sense that, over two seasons, he is slowly letting viewers get to know him better.

That he is clearly more comfortable behind the camera is part of his appeal. In the season one episode "How To Cover Your Furniture," Wilson speaks with an interior decorator about a furniture dilemma he's having. She responds to him—strangely, given the context—like a psychic. Studying him carefully, she makes the observation that he is "always used to having some kind of protective mechanism." She then offers him this piece of advice: "I would love for you, sometimes in your life, in your head, to be like, *I should put the camera down in this situation. I should just be John.*"

### 2.

Wilson is most definitely carrying his camera when I meet him in front of the GameStop in Herald Square. He's hard to miss, in that he's six-foot-two and wearing the khaki hat and jacket I recall from promo images for the show. He's visible in his role as an unassuming documentarian.

I thought he asked to meet outside the GameStop because he wanted to shoot something there, but no. "They

*Illustration by Madison Ketcham*
*Photos by An Rong Xu/HBO, Joe Buglewicz/HBO, and Josh Ethan Johnson/HBO*

don't like it when you film," he says. He's already been thrown out once.

Wilson is looking for particular items today. He pulls out a tiny notebook. I can see words written in the distinctive shaky hand I recognize from the *How To* titles, which Wilson paints himself, using HBO-supplied Wite-Out. The top two items are pictures of women in bikinis, the kind you might find on the wall inside an auto body shop, and clear bottles of piss, often made surreptitiously by bathroom-deprived motorists, who fill them and then fling them out their car windows.

I mention the parallel between this quest and the augmented-reality mobile game *Pokémon Go*, which a few people have been playing in the cold outside the GameStop entrance. Wilson nods, then adds that he hopes that, unlike in *Pokémon Go*, "there is no great programmer dictating what I see."

### 3.

Wilson is thirty-six. At one point during his childhood in Rocky Point, Long Island, he made a movie a day. To say he was devoted to filmmaking is an understatement. He would miss a family vacation in order to finish a movie.

Wilson filmed his creations on a Sony Handycam, which was a gift from Wilson's mother to his father on his father's fortieth birthday. The younger Wilson quickly commandeered the camera. He has remained brand loyal: Wilson now shoots on a Sony FS5, a nice upgrade.

Wilson's early movies belie his later stance as a reluctant performer. They consist primarily of parodies featuring himself, with his name worked into every title, e.g., *RoboJohn* and *John Wars*. He made these films with friends, including Chris Maggio, who now works on *How To* as a camera person.

Maggio was Wilson's partner on *Jingle Berry*, a film they made together at the end of high school, which is highlighted in the season 2 episode "How To Throw Out Your Batteries." Wilson speaks highly of his longtime collaborator, saying, "He shoots the most like me, but also I think he's better than me in a lot of ways, in terms of finding interesting ways to compose images of things you wouldn't think to shoot."

Wilson was also involved in theater when he was younger, playing the lead, Joe Hardy, in his high school's production of the musical *Damn Yankees*. And he was a huge fan of comedian Chris Farley, even going so far as to choose the name Farley as his communion name. He was told he couldn't use it, however, because Farley had just died from a drug overdose.

Wilson mostly avoids theater people in the work he does now, noting that he wants to stay as far from artifice as possible. Also, he is no longer a practicing Catholic.

### 4.

Wilson spent his earliest years in Astoria, Queens, before his father, who had been working in Manhattan as a systems analyst for MetLife, was transferred to Hauppauge, Long Island, and the family relocated to Rocky Point. His mother worked as an educator and then as an administrator in the Rocky Point public schools, which John and his younger brother, Tom, both attended.

His father has great taste in art, Wilson says, recounting how his dad used to take him and his brother to MoMA PS1. When his dad got a DVD player, the first movie he bought, from the used-DVD section at Blockbuster, was Jim Jarmusch's *Stranger Than Paradise*.

His parents are supportive of his work, "but they hold their breath with each episode," Wilson says. He mentions that he tries not to include people he knows in the show to such a degree that it would "ruin my life."

Still, each episode of *How To* includes a memoir component, and the finale of season 2, "How To Be Spontaneous," is arguably one of the most intimate Wilson has thus far made. About a third of the way into it, over anonymous images of people and objects in the city, Wilson unspools the following narration, revealing how some family history is entwined with his approach to documentary:

> When you were growing up, your dad would always try to bring you to places, but they would always turn out to be closed when you got there. This happened so often that he eventually started a blog called *Closed Places*, where he started posting photos of each incident as a way to deal with the pain.
>
> This kind of scared you from making plans, because they never seemed to work out very well. So you just stumbled through life like a piece of driftwood, letting the world shape you instead of trying to control anything. Almost every single thing you've ever recorded is the direct result of randomly being in the right place at the right

time, and it terrifies you to think that you could have missed out on all this great stuff if you had made plans to begin with.

But doing things impulsively doesn't always work out the way you hoped it would, either. Maybe your trip to get a massage was disappointing because you expected it to work out a certain way. And the only way around the family curse is to become a truly spontaneous being and remove anything that even resembles a plan from the equation.

The narration lands on the image of a dead pigeon.

### 5.

In one way, at least, Wilson has always had a plan: to be a great filmmaker. After graduating from high school, he went to SUNY Binghamton to study film. (His buddy Maggio went to Boston University, "the *real* BU," he quips.)

Binghamton's cinema department has a strong history of experimental filmmaking. By the time Wilson got there, he had moved on from making parodies and begun work on original narratives. At Binghamton, he began taking some creative risks. A pivotal moment came when he turned in a short documentary about balloon fetishists, titled *Looner*. "After that, I was hooked," he says.

Wilson did make another scripted film with Maggio after college, when the two reunited and were living in Cambridge, Massachusetts. The movie they wrote, *People Parade*, has some foreshadowing of *How To*'s primary concerns: it's about a low-budget variety show in which Wilson plays the son of the recently deceased host. Filling in for his dad one evening, Wilson introduces a series of increasingly screwball acts while managing several behind-the-scenes disasters.

*People Parade* is funny, but it wasn't fun to make. "It was so stressful for me," Wilson says, "that I decided I didn't really want to do [narrative films] anymore. I never wanted to ask someone to do anything again when I couldn't pay them."

As he was deciding to give up narrative filmmaking, however, his real life was hewing closer to an episode of *How To*. In Cambridge, he had embarked on a job working for a private investigator. His daily commute involved riding his bike to the Red Line; taking the Red Line to South Station; taking the commuter rail to Hanson, Massachusetts; and finally proceeding on foot to a building he describes as a "weird two-story boxy office building in the back of a pizzeria parking lot."

Once there, Wilson climbed up to the second floor, where he sat at a small desk next to his boss's office. Wilson scrubbed footage he had been given, looking for any incriminating moments. He would then export that footage for his boss, who in turn sent it to his clients.

The clients were mostly lawyers focused on issues of workers' comp, so the type of footage Wilson was watching was shot by people who were, for example, wearing hidden cameras into Home Depot, filming someone who should have been in a wheelchair, carrying a two-by-four. "It definitely informed the way that I shoot," he says.

"It felt really exciting even though the stuff was really boring."

After finishing his work early in the day, Wilson spent the rest of his time on the clock watching movies. "I realized that there was a mountain of stuff I needed to watch to become the filmmaker that I wanted to become. So I just spent hours every day watching all the '60s, '70s [films]—like Godard and Cassavetes, just doing the whole chronology, figuring out what I liked and what I didn't like." When not watching films, he took occasional breaks to do push-ups in the bathroom. "I had no future," he says. "All I knew was that I had time."

Wilson was positioned at his desk in such a way that his boss couldn't see what he was doing. "But," Wilson adds wryly, "I feel like they probably had an idea, which is why they eventually fired me and replaced me with a high schooler that they didn't pay."

Some of Wilson's other activities during this time also required him to fine-tune some covert abilities. He remembers pinching copies of this very magazine from a Cambridge newsstand. And he and some friends, occasionally including Maggio, routinely snuck into the Harvard dining halls for free meals.

"There's a special door at Adams House where the ID checker can't see you," he says. "But the students eventually were like, 'Who are these kids? We don't see them in class.' But we became friends with them, and they'd invite us to stuff."

### 6.

Roaming the West Side of Manhattan in the cold, Wilson is looking for his pee bottle Snorlax. He said he's open to suggestions for things to shoot, so I point out a funny-looking tree, but he passes. Later, I show him a doorway where an unfortunate New Yorker appears to have vomited a box of Lucky Charms. He shoots it, noting dryly, "I'm always looking for texture."

We walk farther, and then suddenly Wilson stops in the middle of Forty-First Street, on the west side of Ninth Avenue. I initially don't understand what he's doing, as he stands, back and knees bent, blocking traffic.

But then I see it: the evidence not of the great programmer, but of the Great Programmer. It's a bottle of piss, unmistakably yellow in its repurposed Poland Spring bottle—a little unsung hunk of gold, sitting quietly at the edge of the curb.

### 7.

When Wilson left Cambridge and moved to New York, he began looking for work by searching online for film schools in the city, and New York Film Academy was one of the top hits. Wilson "applied" for a job there using an unusual method: after scouring the web for the name of a department head, Wilson put on some business attire and strode into the NYFA offices, then in Union Square.

He told the receptionist that he had a 2:00 p.m. meeting with the department head, and she called up to see if he was ready. He said he was in a meeting but would see Wilson in fifteen minutes.

"And then I go up," says Wilson. "I think he thinks he forgot about this meeting. And then he asked me what I'd like to do. And I was like, 'Well, I'm really good at editing. I think I'd be a wonderful editing teacher.' And he's like, 'Great. We just let go of our broadcast journalism editing person.'" Wilson took the job.

I express astonishment at how well this scheme unfolded, and Wilson confesses, "I had tried to fake something on a résumé once before and it didn't go well… but this time, it worked." He goes on to acknowledge, "There is this kind of like 'What can you get away with?' mentality that I've had, I think, for a lot of my life."

Wilson stayed at NYFA for about a year before leaving to work as a cameraman shooting informercials, among other things, at a media company on West Thirty-Sixth Street. In the episode titled "How To Put Up Scaffolding," he characterizes his work there as "helping to create some of the most grotesque content on the planet." He took the job initially thinking he would stay there for only one day. Five years later, he was still there.

Frustration with work might ultimately have been the force that helped Wilson make the film that would bring

him to the attention of Nathan Fielder, the comedian and star of HBO's *The Rehearsal*, who is now *How To*'s executive producer.

The impetus for Wilson's life-changing film was a work problem: he had taken a freelance gig making a fashion video, but after a long day of filming and two months of edits, the LA-based client decided that Wilson's film was "unpresentable," and never paid him. When the client stopped returning his calls and then disconnected his number, Wilson took matters into his own hands, bringing the problem to the ultimate arbiter: court TV.

Wilson pitched the case to one court TV show, whose producers informed him that nothing could happen if the defendant refused to cooperate. So Wilson decided to pitch the show again, this time without relying on his former client. Instead, he would dramatize the story, reenacting it with close friends.

Wilson got his friend Clark Filio (now a producer on *How To*) to agree to play the client. He then began contacting more court TV shows, and at last he heard from an LA-based show called *Hot Bench* ("From the producers of *Judge Judy*"!). They asked to see the fashion video in question, so Wilson and Filio dressed up their friend Sharif El Neklawy in "some stylish clothing," and in a few hours, they had put together a (highly amusing) fashion video.

*Hot Bench* took their case. The show booked the "adversaries" on separate flights to LA and in miles-apart hotel rooms. Their appearance is hilarious, in part because Wilson is straining heroically to keep his upper body still. We know why: his

conservative-looking tie contains a hidden camera.

The proceedings are revealed in cuts between the polished show as it was aired to TV viewers and the grainy, haphazard footage as recorded via Wilson's tie. After the judges rule in Wilson's favor, and Wilson and Filio trade (wonderfully faked), bitter post-decision barbs, we finally see Wilson, Filio, and El Neklawy meeting up at a Steak 'n Shake in Santa Monica to celebrate.

But the slightly-less-than-twenty-minute film aims to do more than record a prank. Titled *Los Angeles Plays New York*, it is a riff on *Los Angeles Plays Itself*, a 2003 video essay by Thom Andersen which is constructed entirely of clips from other movies, and which explores the way Los Angeles has been portrayed on-screen.

In *Los Angeles Plays New York*, Wilson observes that despite *Hot Bench* being made in LA, its set and intro were

shot in New York City. Musing on this, he notes that "one day we may all realize that the real New York has become too unrealistic." It's a nice foreshadowing of how he will eventually approach what is *How To*'s ultimate subject: the completely real unreality of New York City.

After Fielder had a chance meeting with Filio, whom he recognized from *Los Angeles Plays New York*, Fielder and Wilson were connected, and the two began to collaborate. Speaking to *The New York Times*, Fielder characterized his role with the show as "trying to help out with whatever." Wilson acknowledges that the two of them have had some heated creative disagreements, but he also notes with gratitude that Fielder "definitely talked me off the ledge a few times."

*Los Angeles Plays New York* was screened at the 2016 New York Film Festival, after which Wilson received a cease and desist order from the fashion client. The film, sadly, is viewable now only if Wilson gives you the Vimeo password.

## 8.

The way *How To* is crafted is highly unusual, in that the script follows the images, not vice versa. Further complicating matters is the fact that most of the images aren't even collected until *after* the writers' room work is complete.

"When you look back at the script after the episode is finished, it's unrecognizable," Wilson says. "Everything needs to be rewritten."

The process goes like this: Wilson comes to the writers' room with seven or eight potential titles for a six-episode season. The writers then generate the material that could be contained under the umbrella of each title, eventually developing a script for each.

The scripts then dictate what the camera people will shoot. At this point, Wilson begins principal photography and records interviews and B-roll every day. At night he "power-scans," as he puts it, through hours of footage that the four separate B-unit teams have shot, which sounds like a gargantuan task. But Wilson sees it differently, characterizing it as "a dream come true. It's like I go out and shoot all day on my own, and then I get this massive dump of some of the funniest, coolest footage in the world. And I get to zone out on my computer and just make selects."

While the assistant editors do the meticulous tagging and key-wording of each shot—which are then put into themed sequences—Wilson's personal project file is much less organized. He usually works from a master sequence that contains every single select of B-roll he has made since the beginning of the show. He refrains from ordering it, because he thinks that's the most inspiring way to look at it: "If I'm having writer's block within the edit, I'll just, like, go in and say, Okay, let me find something that's really funny that I haven't found a home for yet. And then, you know, it has a nice way of, like, jogging your creativity."

As the camera people are shooting, Wilson begins to notice patterns of shots that weren't necessarily called for in the scripts. Once there's two of something, he'll ask the teams to go get twenty more. Sometimes it doesn't turn into anything, but "it's really important to fill out these kind of transitional moments within the episode, because I want the imagery to be really rich, first and foremost."

Given this method, is the writers' room in some ways perfunctory? "I think you ultimately need it," he says. "[Michael] Koman and I put a lot of thought into whether or not a concept is strong enough to carry an episode, and you need to do the writing, even if the script is ludicrous. You need to see if it could be a container for enough funny ideas."

He brings up the example of the episode "How To Appreciate Wine," which started out as "How To Have Taste," before it was decided that the concept needed to be narrowed. "If you start too high off the ground," he says, "it's like there's nowhere else to go."

## 9.

THE BELIEVER: In every episode, you're relying on the universe to present you with some unbelievable imagery. What is your secret to unlocking that? Are you praying?

JOHN WILSON: I don't pray. I just—I believe in, I don't know, the kind of benevolent chaos of the universe that, that just, like, rewards people that just… try a bunch of stuff.

BLVR: [*Laughs*]

---

### VELÁZQUEZ PAINTINGS
### FEATURING A SMALL DOG

✴ *Dog and Cat*, 1650–60
✴ *Joseph's Bloody Coat Brought to Jacob*, 1630
✴ *Philip IV Hunting Wild Boar (La Tela Real)*, 1632–37
✴ *Portrait of Cardinal Infante Ferdinand of Austria with Gun and Dog*, 1632
✴ *Prince Baltasar Carlos in Hunting Dress*, 1635–36
✴ *Infante Felipe Próspero*, 1659
✴ *Las meninas*, 1656
✴ *King Philip IV as a Huntsman*, 1632–33
✴ *Prince Balthasar Carlos Dressed as a Hunter*, 1635–36
✴ *A Buffoon* [incorrectly called *Antonio the Englishman*], 1640
—*list compiled by Katherine Williams*

your partner, you know? It's like that kind of dread.

I try not to think about it that way as much anymore, because it's all just a product of trying. I regret a lot of stuff, but the one thing I never regret is going out to shoot. I know I will come back with something that I just wouldn't have had otherwise. I just try to maximize the opportunities for that once-in-a-lifetime, you know, shot.

### 10.

In Janet Malcolm's book *The Journalist and the Murderer*, there is a line that is reminiscent of the way Wilson's interviewees come across on his show: "People tell journalists their stories as characters in dreams deliver their elliptical messages: without warning, without context, without concern for how odd they will sound when the dreamer awakens and repeats them."

Wilson is in our apartment, petting our family dog, who is also my Pikachu. I ask Wilson if there is anything else he wants to tell the very intelligent readers of this magazine. He considers this for a few seconds, then says. "Uh, there's a hidden joke inside everything. And if you're ever bored, if you stare at something for long enough, you'll find it."

"That's interesting. Do you meditate?"

"No. I should."

"You were raised Catholic," I reiterate.

"Yes, but I didn't learn anything from that," he says.

I mention that staring at something long enough to find the joke hidden within it is a different type of practice.

"Yeah," he says finally. "This kind of work is my religion, I think." ★

JW: I'm trying to think of, like, how to define this. I think the key is just letting people talk, you know, and just continuing to ask questions. Asking questions is just the best way to deal with social anxiety. It's the best way to make documentaries for me. I love Huell Howser's interview style. Do you know him? He is a local California TV personality who would just walk into a restaurant with a microphone and just start asking people what was going on. And he was just, like, so eternally stoked about everything he saw. I love that energy.

BLVR: You said earlier that when you think about how easily you might have missed a particular incredible shot, it's scary. Why is that scary?

JW: Just because, like, I'm just so in love with the thing itself. It would be like thinking about if you never met

# STUFF I'VE BEEN READING

## A QUARTERLY COLUMN, STEADY AS EVER

*by Nick Hornby*

---

**BOOKS READ:**

✶ *Working*—Robert Caro

✶ *Everything's Fine*—Cecilia Rabess

✶ *Empire of Pain: The Secret History of the Sackler Dynasty*—Patrick Radden Keefe

✶ *Ellen and Romeo*—Anonymous

**BOOKS BOUGHT:**

✶ *Working*—Robert Caro

✶ *The Power Broker*—Robert Caro (twice)

✶ *The Years of Lyndon Johnson I: The Path to Power*—Robert Caro

✶ *Pure Colour*—Sheila Heti

---

**I** *think* I have a new literary hero. I cannot yet confirm this, because I have yet to read any of his books—the big ones, anyway—although I have all the best intentions, as you will see from the Books Bought column above. His name is Robert Caro, famous for *The Power Broker*, which is his book about Robert Moses, and his still-unfinished biography of Lyndon Johnson (four volumes to date and counting), and I'm sure you know all about him. He is less known here in the UK: his subject is American power and who ends up wielding it. The British would like to know, for sure, but maybe most of us just want to be told a few names, rather than to be handed a twelve-hundred-page book about someone who has played no part in their lives.

My fascination with Caro began with the documentary *Turn Every Page: The Adventures of Robert Caro and Robert Gottlieb*, which I think every *Believer* reader should see. It's a movie about a writer and his editor, and I hate to be the bearer of bad news, but there is unlikely to be another film in the writer-and-editor genre for the next hundred thousand years. (After that, however, with the way the world is going and all, I expect an unstoppable flood of them.) The editor is Robert Gottlieb, and both men were born in the 1930s—Gottlieb in 1931, Caro in 1935—so there is an undercurrent of melancholy, or at least a sense of time running out, in the documentary. Neither of them knows whether they will be able to finish their work on the last volume of the LBJ series, nor can Caro get a move on. He has to do it his way, with extraordinary thoroughness and patience. Gottlieb is legendary, of course. He worked on Bob Dylan's *Chronicles*, and he discovered Joseph Heller, and he edited John Cheever and Bill Clinton and Katharine Hepburn. Caro, meanwhile, has won two Pulitzers and two National Book Awards; the only historian I have come across with the same ambition, the same inability to leave a stone unturned, is our own David Kynaston, who is in the middle of writing a history of Britain from 1945 to 1979 with astonishing pointillistic detail.

Some of the stories Caro tells in *Turn Every Page* can be found in *Working*, his collection of brilliant essays, and they are stories you can't easily forget. Here's one: Caro wanted to find out more about Lyndon B. Johnson's time at Southwest Texas State Teachers College. He kept hearing whispers that Johnson had stolen a student council election, that he had blackmailed a young female opponent, that he was unpopular, that his college nickname had been "Bull"—for "bullshit"—Johnson. Caro tracked down a classmate, who, unhappy to

*Illustration by Kristian Hammerstad*

talk freely, eventually told him that the information he was looking for was in the 1930 edition of the school's yearbook, the *Pedagog*. Caro, being Caro, had already been through the yearbook and had found nothing illuminating, and asked the classmate to provide page references. She called back with five… but when Caro went back to look for them in his copy, they weren't there. They had been carefully razored out of the book. He tracked down some more copies, in a used-books store in San Marcos, Texas. The first few had received a similar treatment: the pages had been removed. Eventually he found one with the information he needed: proof that Johnson had been loathed by his classmates. There is something both thrilling and chilling about this anecdote. Who removed the pages? How can anyone care this much about preserving a reputation? How does one find copies of a 1930 college yearbook fifty-odd years later, pre-internet?

Caro thought he'd be able to dispense with Johnson's childhood in a couple of chapters, and that he wouldn't have to do much research on it. He went down to Texas a couple of times, but was dissatisfied by the answers he was getting from his interviewees; they were evasive, and they didn't trust him. He decided the only thing to do was to go and live in the Texas Hill Country. As it turned out, he was there for three years. "Why can't you do a biography of Napoleon?" his wife and researcher, Ina, asked him wearily. Caro writes modestly, and with some wry self-impatience—he had no choice but to move to the Texas Hill Country, metaphorically speaking. And even if what interests Caro doesn't interest you, you have to admire his extraordinary commitment to his art. That's kind of what we do here at *The Believer*: admire artistic commitment. *The Power Broker* is seven hundred thousand words long; Gottlieb helped Caro cut another third of a million.

Will I read the Meisterwerke? I'd like to think so, but maybe the time will come only once I have stopped writing this column; otherwise, I'd be telling you stories about Robert Moses and LBJ for the next five years. When you read this, I'll be sixty-six; the melancholy so evident in *Turn Every Page* is contagious. My purchase of *The Power Broker* and the first volume of the Johnson biography is, at the moment, something like the purchase of a football jersey. I am a Caro fan. I am on his team. I want people to know I love him.

Like *Working*, Patrick Radden Keefe's *Empire of Pain* has a recent documentary counterpart, Laura Poitras's great movie about Nan Goldin, *All the Beauty and the Bloodshed*. The Sacklers seem to be, gratifyingly,

## AMERICA'S MOST BANNED BOOKS, BY YEAR

✶ 1992: Scary Stories (series), Alvin Schwartz
✶ 1993–94: *Daddy's Roommate*, Michael Willhoite
✶ 1995: *The Giver*, Lois Lowry
✶ 1996: *The Adventures of Huckleberry Finn*, Mark Twain
✶ 1997–98: *I Know Why the Caged Bird Sings*, Maya Angelou
✶ 1999–2002: Harry Potter (series), J. K. Rowling
✶ 2003: Alice (series), Phyllis Reynolds Naylor
✶ 2004: *The Chocolate War*, Robert Cormier
✶ 2005: *It's Perfectly Normal: Changing Bodies, Growing Up, Sex, and Sexual Health*, Robie H. Harris
✶ 2006–08: *And Tango Makes Three*, Justin Richardson and Peter Parnell
✶ 2009: ttyl; ttfn; l8r, g8r (series), Lauren Myracle
✶ 2010: *And Tango Makes Three*, Justin Richardson and Peter Parnell
✶ 2011: ttyl; ttfn; l8r, g8r (series), Lauren Myracle
✶ 2012–13: Captain Underpants (series), Dav Pilkey
✶ 2014: *The Absolutely True Diary of a Part-Time Indian*, Sherman Alexie
✶ 2015: *Looking for Alaska*, John Green
✶ 2016: *This One Summer*, Mariko Tamaki
✶ 2017: *Thirteen Reasons Why*, Jay Asher
✶ 2018–20: *George* (renamed *Melissa* in 2021), Alex Gino
✶ 2021–22: *Gender Queer*, Maia Kobabe

*—list compiled by Emily Lang*

the most vilified family in the United States right now, although you do seem to have a lot of unspeakable families, so I don't know whether my impression is accurate. I think we can all agree, however, that they have done a lot of unspeakable things. Maybe we can't. Maybe things have become so fractured and fragmented that there is a thriving, angry Sackler Fan Club. Why not, in a country that has warring gun factions? (I'm not claiming any moral superiority for my country, by the way. We have our own unspeakable families and baffling divisions. Are you opposed to traffic in residential streets? Answer yes to that question and you are part of a sinister Stalinist cabal. And you're probably pro-vaccine and anti-Brexit too.)

*All the Beauty and the Bloodshed* gives an enthralling account of Goldin's brilliant and frequently beautiful protest against the Sacklers' creation of the opioid crisis. Keefe's book gives us an enthralling, enraging account of the Sacklers themselves, from patriarch Arthur Sackler's birth, in 1913, to the day in 2021 when Nan Goldin's ferocious campaign resulted in an announcement from the Metropolitan Museum of Art that several of its exhibition spaces would no longer carry the Sackler name. In between is a long, long story, about medicine and the law, greed and cynicism, lies and self-delusion. In other words, it's a Dickens novel, admittedly without too many funny bits, and beyond the reach of satire.

Arthur Sackler worked in pharmaceutical advertising; one of his side projects, publishing a free newspaper

called the *Medical Tribune*, came in especially handy. He could place ads in his publication for the drugs he was representing, and then send it to doctors. When Roche, his main client, introduced Librium and then Valium, his newspaper ran ads for both drugs for decades. Valium and Librium were sold as cures for more or less any nervous condition. Women were aggressively targeted once it was discovered that doctors were prescribing more tranquilizers to them, which is why within a couple of years of the launch of the two drugs, the Rolling Stones wrote "Mother's Little Helper."

But what is really significant about Valium and Librium is the playbook that was devised when it was discovered that they did, after all, create dependency, despite all partisan protestations to the contrary. Addiction, the makers and advertisers of the tranquilizers suggested, was an indication that the user needed *more* of the drug, not less: the discomfort was a sign that the underlying nervous condition had intensified. And in any case, some people had addictive personalities, and would abuse

anything they were prescribed. These arguments would be repeated, word for word, when OxyContin began to destroy millions of American lives. Decades later, Nan Goldin would say that although Arthur Sackler died before OxyContin was unleashed, "he was the architect of the advertising model used so effectively to push the drug… The whole Sackler clan is evil." These views correspond to those of your columnist. Other opinions are available.

Both *All the Beauty and the Bloodshed* and *Empire of Pain* end with a rush of public galleries—the Met and the Guggenheim, in New York, and the National Gallery and the Victoria and Albert Museum, in London, and quite a few more—removing the name of the family that had given them so much money over the years. Even the Sacklers' hedge funds and bankers dropped them. They had squirreled away billions before much of it was taken from them by plaintiffs whose lives had been wrecked by their drugs, and this wealth is a source of great dissatisfaction to campaigners. But their good name was important to them—that's why it was all over many major cultural institutions. (There was nothing they wouldn't sponsor. There was a Sackler Escalator in the Tate Modern.) They are rich, but their name has been ruined for generations. There's something comforting about that. This is the second of two stupendous, definitive books by Patrick Radden Keefe that I've read in the last few months, the other being the sad, gripping *Say Nothing: A True Story of Murder and Memory in Northern Ireland*, about the Troubles. He seems to work faster than Robert Caro, and I for one am grateful.

Cecilia Rabess's *Everything's Fine* is both a love story and a state-of-the-nation novel, and Rabess is so deft in her storytelling and so sly and unshowy in her ambition that you don't realize quite how high she's aiming until you've wolfed the whole thing down. The relationship between Jess Jones and Josh Hillyer begins on the November night in 2008 when Obama was elected. Jess, a young Black woman at an Ivy League college, gives an interview to a student reporter about the momentousness of the occasion, and overhears Josh, the next interviewee, in chinos and a shirt with a collar, talk about the inadvisability of electing a tax-and-spend liberal during a financial crisis. The book ends at the Trump inauguration, with Josh and Jess living together, and watching it together. Whether the relationship will survive the next four years is a question for book groups.

If the novel sounds schematic, or improbable, then I have given the wrong impression. The relationship is messy, unpredictable, and credible, in part, because the world in which Rabess partly sets it is a world she knows something about: Jess and Josh meet again when they are both working at Goldman Sachs, where Rabess was once employed. A lot of first novels, it is fair to say, do not contain authentic-feeling observations of a world the reader knows very little about—my own first novel was about relationships (you've probably been in one yourself) and music (you've probably listened to some). There are so many other strengths to

the writing here, though, that I can almost guarantee that Rabess isn't a one-trick pony—her dialogue is wonderfully sharp and unforced, and she has an ear for conversations that contain meaning and resonance.

Dialogue, it seems to me, is properly valued only in the theater. In films it's regarded as uncinematic ("Too chatty!" a director I was working with kept scribbling on my script); in fiction, ironically, if there's too much dialogue people think you're thinking of the movie rights. Please note, cynical readers: a book with tons of talking in it is *not* a movie, especially if all the talking takes place in the kitchen, over a period of, say, fifty years. Anyway, in this terrific novel, the conversations are a joy. And, yes, someone will option it. I expect they already have. But that's not because Rabess has an ear and discipline. It's because she has something to say, and has found real locations and relationships in which to say it.

I cannot write about the other novel I read recently. I was asked to adapt it (and, yes, it has very good dialogue), but its high-concept twist

makes it unfilmable, I think, because it would necessitate filming the very thing that the author doesn't want you to know. The other way to do it would be to reveal the secret at the same time as all the other characters learn about it, which would render it simply… odd. Let's say this is a novel about an attractive single woman, Ellen, who, despairing of dating apps, falls in love with a giant piece of cheese that she calls Romeo. And while we are led to believe that Romeo is a handsome, unfathomably eligible man—albeit one who could use a new aftershave and crumbles under pressure—everyone else in the book knows that Romeo is a giant piece of cheese, not least because they can see that he's a giant piece of cheese when Ellen takes him to the theater or to a wedding. We can't see this, because we're reading a book that wants to mislead us, and that consists of words, not pictures. The other characters never ask Ellen why she's dating a piece of cheese, because that would give the game away. And then eventually, Romeo gets grilled, or placed between two equally giant slices of bread and smothered in pickles, and we're like, Wait. What? Oh! I get it. *Romeo is a piece of cheese.* I don't know how to turn *Ellen and Romeo* into a movie, even though it's a hugely enjoyable book, so I'm going to have to pass. (The analogy, by the way, is fair.) Anyway, I'm going to be too busy reading *The Power Broker* to do any paid work. That is my commitment to my art—and to you, dear *Believer* reader. You don't even have to read the resulting column, as long as you recognize that. ★

# JULIE OTSUKA

[WRITER]

"YOU DON'T HAVE TO BE A GENIUS TO WRITE, THOUGH SOME WRITERS ARE GENIUSES. YOU DO HAVE TO BE A HARD WORKER."

What Julie Otsuka has learned from twenty years of practice as a writer:
*Don't get stuck polishing sentences*
*The answer may be further down the line*
*Follow the voices*

I first encountered Julie Otsuka—the author and her work—in northwest Pennsylvania in 2009. I had a one-year visiting assistant professorship in fiction at Allegheny College, and Otsuka came through to give a reading. I'd not yet read her debut novel, When the Emperor Was Divine *(2002), about a Japanese American family's forced relocation to a US internment camp after the bombing of Pearl Harbor. Nor had she yet published her follow-up,* The Buddha in the Attic *(2011), about Japanese mail-order brides in the early 1900s, though that night she read aloud an excerpt.*

*Her sentences left me spellbound. Otsuka has a thrillingly unique sensibility, one marked by the enumeration of precise, intimate details. I'd never heard anyone parse the first-person-plural point of view as she does, spinning it out into individual lives and then gracefully gathering them back up. Describing the picture brides' international voyage to the States in* Buddha, *she writes, "Some of us had eaten*

*Illustration by Kristian Hammerstad*

nothing but rice gruel as young girls and had slightly bowed legs, and some of us were only fourteen years old and were still young girls ourselves. Some of us came from the city, and wore stylish city clothes, but many more of us came from the country and on the boat we wore the same old kimonos we'd been wearing for years." By illuminating a range of traits and preferences and experiences, Otsuka not only humanizes the women but ensures this group is not seen as a monolith—an easy assumption about any community.

She takes a similar approach in the opening section of her latest novel, The Swimmers, this time to denote a group of regular visitors to an underground pool. "Most days, at the pool," she writes in the opening pages, "we are able to leave our troubles on land behind. Failed painters become elegant breaststrokers. Untenured professors slice, sharklike, through the water, with breathtaking speed. The newly divorced HR Manager grabs a faded red Styrofoam board and kicks with impunity." The novel ultimately centers on just one swimmer: Alice, an elderly woman in the clutches of dementia.

While Otsuka's narratives span locations and generations— The Swimmers is set more than a century after Buddha— she has several points of consistency. A distinct, authoritative voice, for one. A comprehensive descriptive lens. Measured, metrical prose. She also explores the impact of Japanese Americans' forced imprisonment across books. It's the focal point of When the Emperor Was Divine, in which we follow a family from their comfortable Berkeley, California, home to the Utah desert. They're assigned to "a room in a barrack in a block not far from the fence" and surrounded by machine-gun-carrying guards. They're told they've been brought there "in the interest of national security." They will stay there for years.

Internment is also—spoiler alert—the fate of the picture brides in Buddha, the ultimate betrayal of this promising new world to which they were lured. And in The Swimmers, we learn that as a child, Alice was "sent away to the desert with her mother and brother during the fifth month of that war." These memories buoy up to the surface for Alice, even as so many others submerge into the pool of dementia. "She remembers the scorpions and red ants," Otsuka tells us. "She remembers the taste of dust."

This shameful chapter in American history draws on Otsuka's personal history. Her grandfather, a Japanese American business leader, was named a dangerous enemy alien and arrested by the FBI on December 8, 1941. Her grandmother,

mother, and uncle were relocated to a prison camp. Her grandfather returned in poor health and wasn't able to work again, while her grandmother, who had been a middle-class housewife, became a maid for well-to-do white families. Otsuka said that her mother only occasionally mentioned the camp, and as a girl, the author misunderstood it as a reference to some kind of summer camp.

Born and raised in California, Otsuka received a bachelor's degree from Yale University, and later obtained an MFA in fiction from Columbia University. Her work has garnered significant international acclaim. When the Emperor Was Divine won the Asian American Literary Award and the American Library Association's Alex Award, and was a San Francisco Chronicle Best Book of the Year. The Buddha in the Attic, which has been translated into twenty-two languages, won the PEN/Faulkner Award for Fiction and France's Prix Femina Étranger, and was a finalist for the National Book Award and the International IMPAC Dublin Literary Award. Her other honors include a Guggenheim Fellowship and an Arts and Letters Award in Literature from the American Academy of Arts and Letters.

The author and I spoke in February 2023, three weeks after the White House announced an expanded strategy to address anti-Asian hate, and one week after the American Library Association awarded The Swimmers the 2023 Andrew Carnegie Medal for Excellence in Fiction. The conversation was conducted via Zoom, our voices pinging back and forth between her apartment in Manhattan and mine in Brooklyn.

—Courtney Zoffness

### I. "I CAN'T PAINT, BUT I CAN KIND OF WRITE"

THE BELIEVER: Hi, Julie. Congratulations on the Carnegie Medal. That's so exciting.

JULIE OTSUKA: Thanks.

BLVR: I thought I'd start by talking about your studio arts background. You attended Yale as an undergraduate. I read that you surprised yourself by majoring in studio art. I also studied studio art as an undergraduate. How would you characterize your artistic style back then?

JO: How would I characterize my style back then… you mean my general artistic style?

BLVR: Yes, your visual arts style.

JO: I was learning, so I think I was too young to even have a style. My first love was figurative sculpture. It was just about learning how to see, how to look. The first thing we ever sculpted was a cow femur bone. It was a bone from an animal that was this really abstract thing. It was a great way to learn how to look, because you have no preconceived idea of what a bone should look like, whereas if you're looking at a human head, you do, or think you do, have an idea of what it should look like. This bone was such a complex, gorgeous, beautiful structure that had all these complicated twists and turns in space. I didn't have a style; I was just looking and looking and looking and trying to see. Actually, I think I did have a style without realizing it. I remember my sculpture teacher—he really liked my work and I think he could see, even from the way I sculpted the bone, how I would do the figures, which I went on to do. He could just tell. It's interesting. I would say my style was kind of pared down, which is kind of the way my writing is. [*Laughs*] But my painting… I tried so hard for so many years to be the painter I wanted to be, but there was a big gap between what I wanted to do and what I actually could do. I would not say it was a pared-down style. I was interested in color and some of the abstract expressionist painters from the 1950s. It was a completely different world from the world of figurative sculpture. So yeah. I never really arrived at a style. I was just learning and looking.

BLVR: After college you tried to pursue painting in a more serious way—to become a professional painter?

JO: I wasn't even trying to pursue it professionally; I was just trying to become a better painter. At a certain point I think I realized that I didn't quite have it. I think there was something holding me back psychologically from being the painter I wanted to be. I know I had a gift for color. I know I had a good eye and a good hand. I just became very self-conscious at a certain point and it really made it difficult to go on. I was never able to quite work that out.

BLVR: What you're saying reminds me of what I've heard from some aspiring writers who read masterful books, and rather than feeling nourished or inspired, they feel intimidated to the point of, Well, here's a book that shows me what I can't do, so I may as well do something else. Right? Self-consciousness, too, can be a real inhibitor for writers.

JO: It can be really paralyzing. With sculpture, early on, it was clear that I was very good. With painting, it was maybe clear to some people but it wasn't clear to me initially. It was just something I loved, loved, loved doing. I loved working with paint and oils and color—it's gorgeous, magical stuff. And it's interesting to hear you say that about writing. With writing, I didn't have that. I began writing because it was something I just enjoyed doing. I never, ever thought, when I took my first writing classes, that I would end up being a professional or even a published writer. I was doing it because I liked it. I've always been very process-oriented, which has served me well in some instances; it freed me up and allowed me to make mistakes. I wasn't expecting to be great or even very good, especially initially. I had a greater ease with language than I did with paint. It came more easily to me. It was a fallback, you know? It's like, I can't paint, but I can kind of write. I guess what you're saying is that for many people, writing is to them what painting was for me.

BLVR: Exactly. I think if you aspire to be a certain kind of artist and you believe the gap between your abilities and your models is too large, maybe it intimidates as opposed to encourages.

JO: Right. But especially for students, the gap is always going to be huge in the beginning. It takes years to learn your craft. I didn't publish until I'd been writing for, like, ten years. I think that young people especially shouldn't be intimidated. Easy for me to say, right? I think you also have to be in love with language.

BLVR: For sure. I met an editor years ago who told me—I'll never forget this—that for her, language "goes in one eye and out the other." I was horrified.

JO: I don't even understand what that means. That she doesn't really care about the language? She's only reading for plot?

BLVR: That's how I understood it. Like you, I think being

in love with language is essential to writing a certain kind of book.

JO: Yes. And you also have to be able to be alone. There are many, many months, years, decades, with yourself, in your head.

## II. "A ONCE-A-DECADE NOVELIST"

BLVR: I want to address what you said about it taking ten years before you published anything. There's a lot of pressure on authors to keep publishing. I think this comes from literary professionals who want to capitalize on art, but also from an eager reading public. When I was on book tour in 2021, I kept being asked—and this will undoubtedly sound familiar to you—what I was working on next. It's a question that presumes constant productivity. You've described yourself as a "tortoise," someone who works slowly. I'm wondering about the standard against which you're measuring your own pace. How do you see the relationship between art and speed?

JO: [*Laughs*] I think a book takes as long as it takes. With my books, especially for my first two novels, I did a ton of historical research. I had to know everything about what I was writing about, not before I began to write—I would often research as I was writing—but I was constantly absorbing all this data and keeping notebooks and notebooks filled with facts. It's very time-consuming. I'm also just a really slow writer. Many of us writers are perfectionists. It's hard for me to move on until I've nailed the paragraph. I think I'm a little looser now in my approach and I'm better able to draft out an arc of something—chapter, story, essay— without having to get every paragraph right before moving on to the next one. But my pace is slow. I always thought of myself as a hard worker, but I stopped going to my neighborhood café when the pandemic started, and I began writing a lot at home, which I had not done for, I don't know, thirty years. I had gone to this café every day and that was my writing space. I realized I was a lot more productive at home, which surprised me. It's not what I expected; I love working in public spaces. I was like, Oh, I can work even harder if I stay home!

BLVR: Or faster.

JO: Yeah. I wrote the last chapter of *The Swimmers* in the first year of the pandemic, which for me is super-fast. I mean, I could spend a couple of years writing a chapter. Recently, I've been working on a piece and there's a deadline, and knowing that I have that deadline has been really good. It puts the fire under me. There have been no deadlines for my novels, so I just take as long as I need to take, but I would like to speed it up a little. [*Laughs*] I guess at this point, I am a once-a-decade novelist, but I'd be happy with being a once-every-eight-years novelist. I mean, I'm always making wrong turns and then trying to back out and it takes me a while to figure stuff out. I don't usually begin with a clear idea of where I'm going to end up. I don't outline. I don't have plots. I might sometimes have a general idea, but sometimes I don't; I just need to start writing. It could be a voice that I heard that gets me started and I follow it. There have been times when I've been stuck, more so with my previous books. What I've learned from twenty years of practice of being a writer is that sometimes if I'm stuck, instead of continuing to work at it, I can skip over the stuck place and move on to whatever comes after and then keep moving forward. At some point, I can go back and fill in whatever wasn't working. Sometimes a solution has appeared further on down the line, and I can go back and write it then. In the past, I often got stuck polishing sentences, which is not really writing but is a way of faking yourself into believing that you are. I try not to do that as much.

BLVR: I really relate to that. I have friends who don't re-read what they've written the day before, to avoid the urge to polish, but that sounds hard to do.

JO: Oh, I always start from the very beginning and I read up to where I am, which means that the first few paragraphs are really tightly polished. Then the further you get, it's a little looser.

BLVR: I want to ask about pace more broadly—not just the pace at which you write, but narrative pace. A lot of your stories rebuff conventional plots but still maintain momentum. There's a rhythm to the prose, a repetition that pulls readers through. I wonder how you think about narrative pacing.

## TABLE OF MEN
*by Ama Codjoe*

What I want from you has little
to do with sex, though it, like wine
and bread, rests on the table between us:
the curse that escapes your craned
neck; the way you turn away in bed,
your tongue an animal; and all
the exchanges of power and light.

Nothing of the lies we tell with silence
or the creaking we make as bent pines.

I want the open air of quiet: assured,
azure, birdless—and knowledge
earned from attention.

I'm not your mother, mistress, concubine,
or slave. I want to dine with men
whose kindness hasn't been beaten out, or
who've called it back like the One Lost Thing.
Whose humiliations beget the softening
of eyes. I want to be surprised.

All my life, I've studied you—a matter
of survival. I want not to know you
so well. Here at this table is tenderness,
broken so we might share it.

---

JO: I don't really. I don't think about narrative pacing at all. You mean like when things should happen?

BLVR: I think of pace and momentum as cousins, so the speed at which a story moves forward. Your stories aren't linear or necessarily building toward a climax.

JO: They're more collage-like. In parts of *The Swimmers*, there are a lot of flashbacks, a jumping back and forth, which didn't happen so much with my last novel, although sometimes one of the picture brides would have a memory and flash back to a memory. I just try to keep moving forward in time with each chapter. That's about as structured as I get in terms of narrative momentum. And I try to keep it interesting. Some part of my brain is always paying attention to the rhythm of the language, which I guess can be propulsive and drive the reader to read on, but that's intuitive. I do that without realizing I'm doing it. I'm hooked into the rhythm of sentences.

### III. INTUITION

BLVR: I recently read an essay by Haruki Murakami called "Abandoning a Cat," and there's an interesting moment in which he speaks about intuitiveness.

JO: I've not heard of that essay! I love his work.

BLVR: I do too. The piece is classically Murakami-esque with its curious turns and the way things remain a little mysterious and opaque. I like how his writing plays with a reader's expectations.

JO: I remember when I read one of his first short stories in *The New Yorker* many, many years ago. It was called "Sleep." It blew me away. Amazingly, he inhabits the mind of this housewife who is extremely agitated and unable to sleep. It was unlike anything I'd ever read before, and it was one of the first stories of his ever to have been published in this country. It was quite amazing.

BLVR: Ooh, I want to read it. "Abandoning a Cat" is about his father and their difficult relationship—how essentially they became estranged. Murakami's mother used to tell him, "Your father's very bright." The author writes, "How bright he really was I have no idea. Frankly, it's not a question that interests me much. For somebody in my line of work, intelligence is less important than a sharp intuition."

JO: Oh, that's interesting. Did he mean an intuition about people and how the world works, or did he mean an intuition about what naturally serves the narrative of his story?

BLVR: I took it to mean some kind of narrative intuitiveness.

JO: I've never taught writing, but intuition is something that would be very hard to teach.

BLVR: I also think intuition is its own kind of intelligence.

JO: Well, Murakami's being falsely modest, because obviously he's intelligent. But you don't have to be brilliant to write. You don't. You don't have to be a genius to write, though some writers are geniuses. You do have to be a hard worker. If I start something, it's usually a mess in the beginning, but I'm willing to go back again and again and again. I guess I can understand what he's saying about intuition in terms of how I just know when I've nailed something—when a paragraph finally sounds right. It really has to do with sound. It sounds right.

BLVR: Do you read aloud as you write?

JO: I did a lot with *The Buddha in the Attic*. With *The Swimmers*, I thought, it's kind of like polishing: it's a way of faking yourself into thinking that you're doing work when you're actually wasting half an hour reading out loud. [*Laughs*] I know that when I'm reading silently in my head, I'm still hearing the rhythm, so I don't necessarily need to read aloud. I might at the very end, and also sometimes when I have trouble focusing and I can't hear the language in my head as I'm reading. There are times when I can't hear the thing—then I will read it out loud so I can literally hear it. I need to be able to hear it in my head.

BLVR: Are endings intuitive to you or do they pose a challenge? Does the absence of a conventional plot make the final sentiment harder to locate?

JO: It depends. I knew when I started writing *The Buddha in the Attic* what that last chapter would be. It was a piece of unfinished business that I hadn't dealt with in my first novel. I always wanted to know: What did the mostly white folks in these towns think after their Japanese neighbors suddenly disappeared overnight? I never had a chance to deal with that, really. I wanted to explore their point of view, so I knew that would be my ending point. I also like a twist at the very end of a novel, like suddenly shifting from the point of view of the Japanese picture brides to the point of view of this white

town. So I knew that. With my first novel, *When the Emperor Was Divine*, I didn't know how I would end the book. I knew I wanted to account for the father's voice in some way, but I didn't know what form his voice would take, and it took me a while to figure that out. And with *The Swimmers*, I think I found the ending. It was more like a reshuffling of scenes. I suddenly saw this scene and I thought, Oh, this would actually be great at the very end—I could have it at the end as a flashback. I knew it was an emotionally moving, hot moment to end on, so that's why I put it there as opposed to tucking it somewhere in the middle of the chapter.

## IV. CONDITIONAL PRESENCE

BLVR: Your work illuminates hostility toward Japanese Americans before, during, and after the Second World War. You describe internment and dramatize it, but you also consider a variety of ways our society devalues or rejects immigrants. You and I are speaking amid an enormous surge in anti-Asian violence in this country, which may be attributed to the pandemic's purported origins in China. I'm wondering how you square the kind of racism you explore, some of it a century old, with what is happening today.

JO: I never thought I would see what I'm seeing now in my lifetime. I was born in the 1960s and the demographics of this country were different. It was a very, very white country back then. I don't want to get into the details of immigration history, but there was a 1965 immigration act, which allowed many more people from Asia to come over. Just a handful of Asians could come in every year after 1924 until 1965. When I was growing up, there were not many people who looked like me or my family—I grew up in Palo Alto—but we were treated well. As I grew older, there were more and more people who looked like me, because there were more and more immigrants coming over from Asia. The visual landscape really changed. I guess I'm saying I never encountered a lot of racial hostility. I was teased as a kid in the schoolyard, but that's totally normal, I think. I was able to brush that off. I remember on my first day of school, my mother said, "If anyone teases you, just ignore it." And I did, basically. I don't know. I think I had a strong sense of self. I think that's something my mother instilled in her kids. If somebody said something to me or teased me, I kind of wrote it off. I was able to tell myself, It's their problem.

BLVR: You mean if someone teased you in a racist way?

JO: Yeah. You know, making "slant eyes" or just saying stuff on the playground. I didn't let it bother me. I never felt less than and I always had a lot of friends. I didn't feel bullied. It did happen, but I don't feel traumatized or anything by it. Generally, I felt very accepted by my classmates. I never felt that I was in danger until the pandemic started. It was shocking to see this sudden upsurge of anti-Asian hate. I was glad, in a way, that my mother wasn't around to see this. If something had ever happened to my parents… it would have just killed me, even just to see them mocked. I don't know what I would do. It would just really, really—that would hurt. I feel I could take it, but to see something happen to my parents, especially my mother, after everything she'd gone through, that would have been hard to take.

BLVR: Because she was in an internment camp during the war.

JO: Right, right. I just would not want anyone to mess with her. It makes you realize how conditional your presence is in this country. You can think you're doing fine, you're blending in, whatever, you're one of us, and then something like the pandemic happens and suddenly the rug is just pulled out from under you. In the first days of the pandemic, I remember walking out of my building and I'd never felt so self-conscious about being Asian. It was the weirdest thing. I was aware of looking like someone who could possibly be carrying the virus and not knowing what people would think. That was very odd. It's very weird. I'd never experienced that before.

BLVR: I'm sorry. I can't imagine. *When the Emperor Was Divine* resurfaced in the national news this past summer, when a Wisconsin school board in the Muskego-Norway district banned it from being taught to a tenth-grade English class. I read an article in which school board members supposedly called the book "too sad," and also claimed that it lacked an "American perspective." Of course, so many of the families

---

### FEMALE AUTHORS WHO ORIGINALLY PUBLISHED UNDER MALE PSEUDONYMS

✶ Charlotte Brontë—Currer Bell
✶ Anne Brontë—Acton Bell
✶ Emily Brontë—Ellis Bell
✶ Mary Ann Evans—George Eliot
✶ Louisa May Alcott—A. M. Barnard
✶ Helen Lyndon Goff—P. L. Travers
✶ Amantine Lucile Aurore Dupin de Francueil—George Sand
✶ Katherine Harris Bradley and Edith Emma Cooper (together)—Michael Field
✶ Elizabeth Gaskell—Cotton Mather Mills
✶ Violet Paget—Vernon Lee
✶ Agatha Christie—Monosyllaba
✶ Ann Petry—Arnold Petri
✶ Nelle Harper Lee—Harper Lee
✶ Karen Blixen—Isak Dinesen
✶ Princess Zeb-un-Nissa—Makhfi

✶ Mary Bright—George Egerton
✶ Natsuko Higuchi—Ichiyō Higuchi
✶ Frances Rollin Whipper—Frank A. Rollin
✶ Doris Boake Kerr—Capel Boake or Stephen Grey
✶ Edith Maude Eaton—Sui Sin Far
✶ Frances Tiernan—Christian Reid
✶ Mary Hawker—Lanoe Falconer
✶ Julia Frankau—Frank Danby
✶ Pearl Richards—John Oliver Hobbes
✶ Mary St. Leger Kingsley—Lucas Malet
✶ Violet Nicolson—Laurence Hope
✶ Julia Constance Fletcher—George Fleming
✶ Alice Dunbar Nelson—Monroe Wright
✶ Aubertine Woodward Moore—Auber Forestier
✶ Mary Gludd Tuttiett—Maxwell Gray
✶ Margaret Fairless Barber—Michael Fairless
*—list compiled by Emily Lang*

relocated to internment camps were American citizens. I wonder what this banning has meant to you and your work.

JO: Well, it was a shock, for one thing. I travel across the country speaking to college students mostly, and mostly about that book. I had never encountered any sort of pushback at all. I was really surprised initially. And it made me very angry. It made me even more determined to get this story out there. I still meet so many young students who've never heard anything about the Japanese American incarceration—even now. Twenty years ago, I thought, Well, twenty years from now, everybody will know, but so many young kids still don't know. I thought there would be more fiction written about the camps, but there isn't a lot out there. Still. I'm not sure why.

BLVR: I was going to ask how you understand this.

JO: I don't know if it's because Japanese Americans are not writing about this? There have been a lot of documentaries, but I don't know. Or is it the publishing houses? I don't have an easy answer. It made me realize it's more important than ever to keep this story out there. My book is one way of keeping the story alive. But I never thought it would come to this. I just didn't. What was amazing, though, was to watch these local townspeople, parents, teachers, and students rally around the book in support of it, against the ban. That was an amazing and beautiful thing to watch, because this is a very conservative town. It was unusual in that most book bans are initiated by parents in the community. This ban was initiated by school board members, not by the parents in the town, and there was a rally where I think 150 people showed up. Former students from this high school spoke out in defense of free speech and I thought, This would not have happened eighty years ago, when the evacuation orders were first posted on signposts telling the Japanese Americans they had to leave. Nobody came to our defense then.

BLVR: It's double-edged.

JO: Yes, it is. I mean, the rally gave me hope, but also just, What?! I mean, I know it's part of this nationwide movement to erase certain histories from the official record. I understand that. I don't know why, but I didn't think it would happen to my book. Until it did.

BLVR: America behaving badly seems to be a common denominator among book bans. Ugly history.

JO: Yeah.

## V. CALIFORNIA AS LANDSCAPE

BLVR: *The Swimmers* features an underground pool in an unnamed California suburb. *The Buddha in the Attic* opens with a boat ferrying picture brides to San Francisco Bay. And *When the Emperor Was Divine* dramatizes the experience of a Japanese American family who were forcibly removed from their home in Berkeley. Artists often use California as a metaphor for the American dream—it was the site of the Gold Rush, et cetera. But as you alluded to earlier, you were born and raised there. Can you speak to how place informs your work? Does California as an idea or an ideal ever factor into your thinking when you set a story?

JO: You know, I don't even think of California as an idea. I think of it visually, as a landscape. It's the landscape that imprinted upon me as a child. It's a beautiful place—just gorgeous. I have very fond memories of growing up there. It was a great place to have an outdoor, kind of free-range childhood. So there's that. But I guess it is where my ancestors came to begin their new lives, so it was for them a state of promise. I haven't lived there for thirty-five years, but it's still the landscape that is most vivid for me, and the place that I just keep going back to.

BLVR: Do you miss living there?

JO: You know, I love living in New York City. I can't imagine myself living anywhere else. My father died in 2021 and then the house was sold and it's very weird to realize, Oh, there's no home to go back to. It's very, very final when your parents are gone and your childhood house is gone. I still have family out there, and I miss things like the smell of the ocean. I mean, I know there's an ocean on the East Coast too…

BLVR: It's not the same.

JO: It's not. And the light out there, it's just gorgeous. So yeah, I think I miss it, but not enough that I need to move out there and leave New York City.

BLVR: I have another question about a potential metaphor or idea. When a crack appears on the pool floor in *The Swimmers*, there are all these theories around its origins and implications. You've said that you invented this crack as a metaphor for a rupture, a sudden break in reality, and the theme is echoed in the novel's subsequent section with Alice's disappeared memory—a personal rupture. I wondered if cultural or political circumstances also informed your desire to explore this break in reality. I couldn't help but think that when the novel discusses the "crack deniers."

JO: [*Laughs*] I wrote that chapter before the pandemic. And I don't think I began writing about the crack as a metaphor. I began writing it as this unexpected interruption on the bottom of this community pool. I began writing about it in a literal way—it was a literal presence initially. But then things kind of spun out of control. [*Laughs*] I realized, Wow, I could really go to town with this crack.

BLVR: That's the best. I feel the fun you're having on the page.

JO: It was fun. In some places, things even got a little silly. It's funny, some of the foreign translators of the novel will say things like "There is no Ivalo mutation" [a condition one patient at Alice's memory care facility suffers from]. And I'm like, That's because it's fiction; there isn't one. I just made up that mutation. That's one thing that stands out, but a lot of the science in *The Swimmers* is completely invented. These studies are things I made up.

BLVR: Ah, to be a fiction writer.

JO: Right! [*Laughs*] But, yeah, the crack deniers. I'm sure

that whatever was going on at that current moment in politics was somehow seeping its way into what I was writing. But it was definitely pre-pandemic.

BLVR: I read that you don't own a TV. True?

JO: That's true.

BLVR: Do you watch anything on your laptop?

JO: I do, yeah. [*Laughs*]

BLVR: Do you have a favorite show?

JO: I love *The Americans*. Did you see that?

BLVR: I didn't. I should.

JO: It's some of the best TV I've ever seen in my life. It's amazing. And that they could keep it going for seasons and seasons and seasons. It's really stunning. And I love *The White Lotus*. I thought it was great.

BLVR: It's so good. So juicy.

JO: Yes, yes. And the last season ended with that perfect operatic arc.

BLVR: Literally, an arc right off the boat!

JO: Exactly! It was a great ending. So yeah, I watch some TV.

BLVR: Well, I appreciate your time and thoughtfulness—and your work. Per the earlier question about pacing and the time it takes to write, anyone should be so lucky to write a book as beautiful as one of yours.

JO: Oh, thank you.

BLVR: I mean, what's ten years? A blip!

JO: [*Laughs*] Yeah, but then the blip's up and suddenly it's all over and it's like, What did I do with my time on this earth? You know? ★

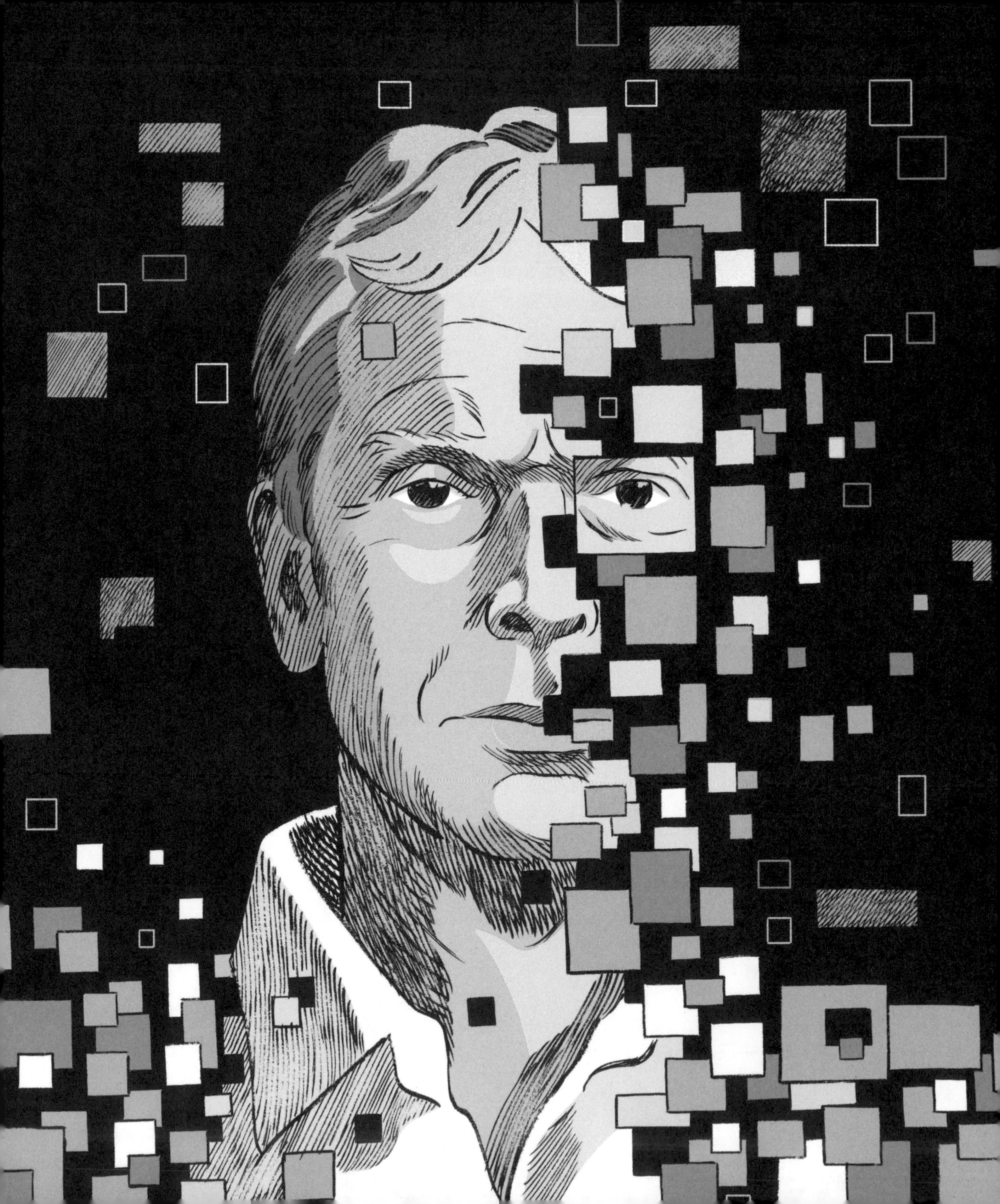

# ADAPTIVE FICTIONS

*In Irvine, California, one cognitive scientist has put forth a new theory of perception, which suggests, among other things, that he doesn't have a brain.*

*by* **TED McDERMOTT**                    *illustrations by* **ANDREA SETTIMO**

## I.

I was, let's say, having a bad day when I came across Donald Hoffman in the stacks of the downtown Spokane Public Library last summer. Not that anything was really wrong. Only that I was unemployed and weeks away from turning forty. Only that middle age was here and it was hard to believe I was still *here*: exhausted and uninspired in the long shadow of the pandemic, trying to keep my kids occupied on yet another scorching afternoon of yet another climate-change summer, in a midsize city where I knew almost no one. Only that I lived with my family across a dirt alley from a liquor store and saw, almost every time I looked out our living room windows, someone shooting up or heating up aluminum foil and inhaling or hallucinating or peeing or fighting or starting a fire. Only that the detritus of this chaotic survival—uncapped needles and disassembled pens, plastic spoons and spent condoms, half-drunk Mountain Dew bottles and empty Cup Noodles containers—kept accumulating in my backyard. Only that amid all this I was trying, of all the things I could've been doing, to do what I am always trying

to do: redeem my reality by converting it into fiction.

My kids, however, made different demands. I had taken them to the library to keep them entertained, and now they wanted to go to the play area. I asked that they please just give me one minute to try and find something to read. This should've been easy, but even books—one of the few things I had thought mattered to me—no longer held my attention, because whatever I picked up seemed to me like the playing out of some form or style that had been set long ago and exhausted soon after, like a superficially new way of essentially describing the same thing: life and its various discontents. So I suppose I saw the title running down the spine of Donald Hoffman's book *The Case Against Reality* as something like a lifeline, a comprehensive promise to escape what was bothering me, which happened to be absolutely everything.

But when I started thumbing through its pages on the periphery of the play area, I realized this was the opposite of what I'd assumed: it was not a lifeline but a rope ladder dropped into a rabbit hole, where, I found, I was happy to go. Here was Hoffman, my White Rabbit, asking, *What happens when you open your eyes and feel you're alive? Are you right to assume that your sensations correspond to an objective, external reality? That these sensations help you to navigate the objects that make up the world? That objects do, in fact, make up the world? What if*, Hoffman wanted me to wonder, *you don't see what's actually out there at all?*

This was a book of science, which I know nothing about, but I could

already see that it was investigating a question I'd only ever thought to wrestle with in fiction: What is the relationship between the person you believe yourself to be and the reality you perceive?

There was something different, too, about Hoffman's approach to this whole question. What I had seen only as a matter of personal struggle, Hoffman was effusively describing as an exciting opportunity to rethink the very nature of being alive.

"The delight of mystery," he wrote, "which we sometimes fetch from the netherworld of a black hole or a parallel universe, can be enjoyed, here and now, in your very chair."

At the moment, my chair, as it were, resembled a cartoon of a log: a plastic bench that looked as if it had been lifted from an illustration in a children's book. Meanwhile, my daughter and son were on the far side of the play area, dragging a bunch of beanbags into a pile, so they could climb up high onto some foam risers, jump off, and softly land. It was on this log—this thing both solid and somewhat imagined—that I journeyed through quotes from Galileo, references to *The Matrix*, and bewildering math, all in service of Hoffman's contrarian case: that nothing is what it seems to be.

What appear to be the people, places, and things of external reality, he argues, are all entirely illusory. What seems like being alive is actually like being inside a virtual reality designed by evolution to keep us alive. What underlies reality are not the forces and masses of physics but the meldings and mergings of consciousnesses. What looks like a fundamental distinction between the spiritual and the scientific is simply a relic of our inability to drop our preconceptions and think clearly.

He acknowledges that it all might sound "faintly mad," but Hoffman is unwavering in his conviction that we are seeing everything wrong, no matter how hard it is for even him to believe—and even though his own theory puts him in the unlikely position of being a cognitive scientist who believes brains do not exist.

It was the kind of belief that would ordinarily require faith: that the world is a veil we must lift to see the fundamental truth that originates in a singular consciousness. But Hoffman's proof exists in math rather than in scripture, and it might one day be able to account for everything physical and mental: from time and light and mass to the taste of chocolate and the feeling of love and the sensation of sitting on a cartoon log, reading a book about how the world that you think exists can be proved to be an illusion. Hoffman is adamant that his theory is just where logic would lead anyone willing to follow it to its limit: to the startling conclusion that reality is lying to you in order to help you survive.

I had long been interested in the usefulness of not telling the truth, of trying to convert the baffling thrum of being alive into a fictional narrative in which everything teemed with meaning, but my efforts had served mostly as a Rube Goldberg machine for my mind: a needlessly complicated contraption for dealing with the reality in front of me by not dealing with it at

all. But when the pandemic descended, reality became impossible to ignore. Personal and external chaos seemed to be besieging me. And increasingly, my reality seemed to be urgently saying something to me—seemed to be flashing me a warning, alerting me that I had come to the wrong place, and had brought my family there too.

I checked out Hoffman's book and brought it home to read. Over the next few weeks, I became so engrossed in his argument that my wife would sometimes prod me in front of other people: "Go ahead," she'd say, "tell them what you think about reality now."

"Oh, I mean, it's not what *I* think," I would counter, hedging my enthusiasm, afraid I would sound—oh, I don't know—willfully eccentric if I embarked too unreservedly, too unironically, on an impassioned disquisition about how reality is not real. "It's just this weird thing this guy—he's a scientist; he went to MIT—is saying."

"Oh yeah," my interlocutor would say, "and what's that?"

"In the simplest terms," I would offer, sounding insufferable, "it's the idea that physical reality doesn't produce consciousness with the organ of the brain, but the other way around: that consciousness actually *creates* physical reality. Or, more accurately, the illusion of physical reality—the brain included."

But what did I really think? Maybe the source of my uncertainty was all the talk of how unreliable our perceptions are, but I believe it was something more: my ignorance, which forced me into a faith-based relationship with the science Hoffman uses. And when you're relying on faith, you're looking

for signs. But when you are using the internet, you find information, which tended to further my confusion.

I imagined that Hoffman was an esoteric figure, an abstruse thinker, and that I therefore was the same—or at least similar. But when I googled him, I discovered I was one of millions of people who'd watched his TED Talk, who'd listened to his countless podcast appearances, who'd seen his discussion with Deepak Chopra, who had at least a passing interest in the possibility that science shows us that reality is illusory.

I was less interested in what all this meant about Hoffman than in what it said about me, and I feared it said I'd been duped. But because I couldn't see myself with any objectivity, I was in search of a judgment of Hoffman. Was he faintly mad? Or was he totally mad? Or was he a total genius? Since the answer wasn't forthcoming from afar, I decided I should meet him myself—see for myself.

It was fitting that we met first in an interface, in a Zoom room, and that Hoffman was somewhere I'd seen him before, in some of the many YouTube videos I'd watched: sitting before a blank wall, with a fake orchid on one side and a neat arrangement of what appeared to be his three published books on the other, in a space with as much personality as a dentist's office. I thought it was a real room, but only later did I realize it was an illusion, a virtual background that replaced the reality of wherever he really was.

As for me, I had donned a collared shirt in my dining room and attempted to project that I was serious. As we talked, it became clear that even

Hoffman himself had trouble adjusting to the implications of his ideas.

"My own theory just bothers the hell out of me, in terms of what it means personally," he said. "So I don't have neurons? OK, what the hell am I?"

## II.

The body of Donald Hoffman was born in 1955, in an army hospital in San Antonio, to parents who spent their lives wandering the same borderlands where Hoffman has spent so much of his: the place where science and religion meet.

After leaving Texas, his family bounced around Southern California, where his father developed computer technology for the aerospace and defense industries before becoming a fundamentalist pastor at various charismatic churches. Meanwhile, his mother, who Hoffman believes was "pretty close to a genius," studied Christian counseling before working as a church preschool administrator and a programmer at a bank.

"And so it was very, very interesting," Hoffman told me. "On the one hand, Dad's making important technical contributions to the state of the electronics industry. My mom could easily have been a world-class programmer. So they're also interested in the bigger questions, but they were not willing to question the position of the church or the position of the pastors on the bigger questions. Whenever our discussions went that way, there was no freedom to think outside the box philosophically about this stuff. It was by the Bible or not at all."

But whereas his parents were content to keep the scientific and the spiritual in separate but unequal spheres—the former a tool; the latter the truth—Hoffman has worked for decades to use the tool to determine the truth. He doesn't reject religion. Indeed, he knows that his theories are built on a long history of spiritual practice, especially in the East, and a rich vein of philosophical thought, one that passes through pre-Socratics like Parmenides to idealists like Kant to twentieth-century thinkers like Bertrand Russell. But he's adamant that all these ideas are merely that: ideas, speculations, pointers toward truths that they can't actually touch. What Hoffman wants is something else, something novel: a "completely rigorous" and "mathematically precise" scientific theory that makes falsifiable predictions about how the mind makes the material world.

"Someone who's a Hindu or Buddhist could say, *Well, welcome to the party, you latecomers. We've been saying this for several thousand years,*" Hoffman told me. "And I would say, *Yes, but this is the first time it's being said precisely. This is the first time we're saying it in a way that we can actually make mathematically precise predictions, where we can actually see the limits of our pointers.* So everybody's got a piece of the puzzle, and I think collaboration, cooperation, as opposed to building fences and defending turf, is the way forward. But letting go of spacetime is a sine qua non for progress."

You must let go of the conception of spacetime as a foundational, physical plane on which material reality unspools as the seconds tick past—not so you can wipe the veil from your eyes and become enlightened, or because doing so will release you from your delusional materialism. You must let go of the physical world, according to Hoffman, because math and science and logic demand that you do so.

Theories about the nature of reality generally fall into two categories. Dualist ones assume there are two fundamental things: the physical and the spiritual, the corporeal and the mental, the body and the soul. Monist theories, on the other hand, assume only one of these is truly foundational, and the other is merely derivative of what is most basic. Dualism seems more commonsensical; monism has the advantage per Occam's razor, a principle that says a model is more true the fewer assumptions it makes. And for thousands of years, much theological and philosophical debate has centered around which of these models best fits the world. Is it, as Descartes famously conjectured, that reality involves the interaction between matter, which exists in space, and mind, which exists in thought? Or is it, as Leibniz and Hoffman argue, that only mind exists, that what appears to be stable and external is merely a projection of the internal and mental, a phenomenon of perception?

Throughout the twentieth century, a different conviction began to exert more influence, the idea that everything, including the mind, is a product of physical matter. It's an assumption so prevalent in our scientific age that it's hard to realize that anyone's making it. Subatomic particles make atoms, and atoms make objects—including bacteria and galaxies and bodies and brains—and brains make thoughts, and thoughts

**WHAT APPEAR TO BE THE PEOPLE, PLACES, AND THINGS OF EXTERNAL REALITY, HE ARGUES, ARE ALL ENTIRELY ILLUSORY.**

make what we call, not quite knowing what we mean, consciousness.

This belief in a physical monism strengthened in the twentieth century, as computer science produced machines that seemed capable of thinking, and thereby created a mechanistic metaphor for—if not a model of—how the firing of neurons produces our sense that we are perceiving, thinking, living. By 1991, you could slide a human into an fMRI machine and record how various stimuli caused subtle changes in their brain. In this way, the brain became widely understood as the mechanism that produces the mind. It's a concept we mostly take

for granted now, but in 2001 my late uncle, Drew McDermott, a professor of computer science at Yale, "risk[ed] raised eyebrows from [his] colleagues" to pen an entire book that sought to solve "the mind-body problem from a computational perspective." In it, he argues that our brains are a kind of computer and that consciousness is in fact "a necessary component of computational intelligence, not an inexplicable accident."

Hoffman came to share this attitude as he freed himself of the preconceptions of his Christian upbringing and entered MIT, where my uncle also got his doctorate, to study

computational psychology under David Marr, a foundational figure in the field. But despite this transformation, Hoffman maintained a kind of religious ambition to find a framework that would explain not only phenomena but also their common source. In his first year, Hoffman detected that various specific phenomena in visual perception—like how we see a two-dimensional screen in three dimensions, or how we can detect edges in a seamless visual field—could be described with a "similar mathematical structure." So he tried to unify these discrete ideas into a general mathematical theory of

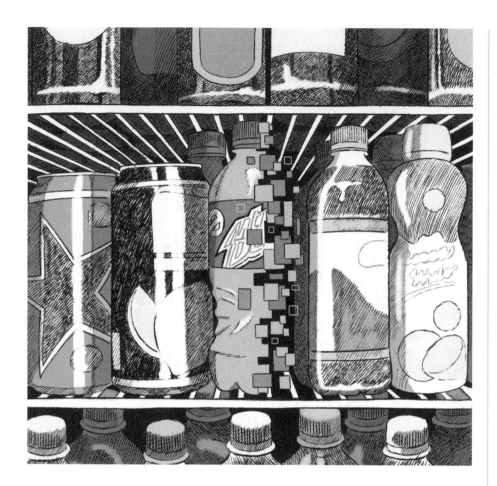

AND SO EVOLUTION BUILT US AN INTERFACE—WHAT WE USUALLY CALL REALITY—THAT CONDENSED AND ENCODED THE RICHER TRUTH INTO A FORM WE CAN NAVIGATE AND MANIPULATE AND BELIEVE IN.

perception—one that offered a comprehensive explanation for how our awareness works.

After he'd drafted a paper proposing such a theory, he brought it to Marr, who immediately identified a basic flaw: Hoffman was using the wrong kind of math. But it was the only math Hoffman knew, so he decided to focus on "specific, concrete problems" with more achievable answers. Hoffman did so—but he let his focus wander after he got a job, in 1983, at the University of California at Irvine, where he has been ever since, pursuing a forty-year quest to finish what he started in his early twenties.

Soon after he arrived on Irvine's circular, modernist campus, Hoffman received an email from Bruce Bennett, a fiery math professor and devout Buddhist who'd also apparently played saxophone with Charles Mingus. When they met for lunch to discuss collaborating, Bennett dispensed with the small talk.

"The first thing he said to me was 'I don't like bullshitters, and if you're a bullshitter, I'm not gonna deal with you,'" Hoffman recalled. "So that was his hello. That was the kind of guy he was."

Bennett, whom Hoffman describes as "unreasonably talented" and "an

unbelievable mathematical genius," had taught at Harvard and Stanford, but his academic career was languishing, as was Hoffman's paper on a general theory of perception. So after Bennett expressed an interest in working together, Hoffman pulled out his draft. Bennett's initial response was the same as Marr's: he pointed out that Hoffman's ideas were interesting, but his math wasn't up to the ambitious task. But unlike Marr, who had died while Hoffman was still at MIT, Bennett "patiently tutored" Hoffman in what he needed to know.

Over the next few years, Bennett, Hoffman, and Chetan Prakash, a mathematician and aikido expert who remains a close collaborator, hunkered down in the building where Hoffman still has a lab, converting Hoffman's interesting questions and creative energy into mathematically precise arguments.

"Often, I would be the one that would have an idea about where we needed to go," Hoffman said. "And they would say, 'Here's the mathematics we would need to do that.'"

While his collaborators were prone to getting distracted and joking around and otherwise wasting time, Hoffman was on a mission. "I was almost like the teacher that was telling the kids, *OK, we need to get back to work*," he recalled.

In 1986, that work paid off, when the math began to show that there is a distinction between reality and perception; when it started to become clear that seeing something doesn't actually require a thing, that the mind doesn't actually require matter in order to perceive. Up until that point, Hoffman had assumed what we all assume: that if we see something, it's because it is there.

"But what our theory was saying was *No, no, no, there's a step in between*," Hoffman told me.

So Hoffman asked Bennett a question: "What is a 'fork' in our theory?" A fork, Bennett said, was not what we all assume it is: a pronged instrument used for eating. And it was not what a physicist might describe it to be: an assemblage of atoms. It was, Bennett told Hoffman, "the conclusion of an inference." It was, in other words, a bit of complicated math performed automatically in the mind. It was, put simply, a thought. And a thought doesn't necessarily depend on anything physical.

And if mind doesn't depend on matter, Hoffman realized, maybe matter doesn't exist at all.

"And that's when I had my epiphany," Hoffman told me. "But I didn't greet it with joy. I was so scared that I had to sit down."

What scared him was what it meant: that the physical monism of his scientific framework, which views mind as matter, couldn't be true; that the opposite, in fact, was more likely: that matter is mind, that the one fundamental element of reality is mental.

"So that was when I had my come-to-monism moment," Hoffman told me.

Three years after his epiphany, Hoffman, Bennett, and Prakash published their findings in a dense, highly mathematical tome titled *Observer Mechanics: A Formal Theory of Perception*. According to Hoffman, the book fleshes out how perception is independent of anything objective out there, and tries to describe mathematically how physics arises from consciousness, though it doesn't use that then-unfashionable term. But even though the authors were arguing for a reimagining of everything, their book didn't exactly make a splash.

"My guess is that there are less than ten people in the world that have read it and understood it," Hoffman told me.

Among the few who absorbed their argument, though, was the quantum physicist John Archibald Wheeler, who cited the book in a landmark paper introducing his "it from bit" concept, which argued, among other things, that the "world cannot be a giant machine, ruled by any preestablished continuum physical law,"

and that there "is no such thing at the microscopic level as space or time or spacetime continuum." The nod from a figure as major as Wheeler made Hoffman "quite happy," but it wasn't enough. He wanted broader recognition for his ideas.

So a decade later, in 1998, Hoffman tried again to make his much-refined case, publishing a second book, *Visual Intelligence: How We Create What We See*. This time, Hoffman tried to make his ideas more accessible, leaving out the equations entirely and waiting to spring his wholesale dismantling of reality on the reader.

"I tried to make a respectable book," he told me, "but then the punch line is at the end."

And the punch line of the final chapter is a radical one: that life "is all virtual reality." A year later, a movie came out with the same punch line. "So you can imagine I was all over *The Matrix*," Hoffman told me. "I thought it might help turn the tide, but it didn't."

Hoffman, characteristically undeterred and single-minded, spent the next decade trying to show his colleagues why he had to be right.

"I realized there's only one way I'm going to stop my colleagues in their tracks, and that's to prove, if possible, that evolution entails that this is a virtual reality," he said. "I realized that if I can prove that, they can no longer dismiss me."

He set out to do so with math, with something called evolutionary game theory, which allows a researcher to assign points to different adaptations and to determine the odds of each winning in a hypothetical game. And, incredibly, it worked. It turned out, according to Hoffman's peer-reviewed research, that when he pitted fitness against truth in such simulations, when he and his collaborators asked whether an organism would earn more points if it prioritized accuracy or survival when it perceived, survival won over and over again. Not only that, but these simulations showed something even more counterintuitive: that truth and fitness are opposed, that "seeing truth hides fitness, and seeing fitness hides truth."

And so evolution built us an interface—what we usually call reality—that condensed and encoded the richer truth into a form we can navigate and manipulate and believe in. Perception, in other words, conceals the truth of reality in order to aid us in our survival. What we see is not accurate—but it's not arbitrary either. It is something to be taken "seriously, but not literally." It should be viewed like an icon on a desktop or an avatar in a VR headset: laden with meaning but entirely artificial; a construct that "guides adaptive behavior"— that helps us, in short, to reproduce.

Everything physical is like this, according to Hoffman's theory: expressive of something deeper. A beanbag, for example, is a symbol that evolution encoded to efficiently package information about how to soften your landing and keep you from harm. And it's not just a beanbag, of course. A library, a cartoonish log, a book about reality, a spent condom, a half-drunk Mountain Dew bottle, a high-rise hotel with dirty windows, a Lyft driver in a Tesla— nothing is what it seems to be, because everything in Hoffman's confounding worldview is an "adaptive fiction," a useful lie.

## III.

As Hoffman and I continued our talks, and as his ideas, increasingly, became mine, I began, strange to say it, adopting Hoffman as a kind of spiritual guide, though I couldn't shake the feeling that I was making an obvious mistake, that I was only in thrall to his theories because I didn't have the expertise to evaluate them. Maybe this was all pseudoscience, I thought, a sort of religion of the metaverse. But when I broached the idea that maybe this wasn't as scientific as he wanted it to be—was perhaps more religious than he wanted to admit—Hoffman pushed back.

"Some say, *Well, Hoffman's proposing postmodernism here and deconstruction, and he's let go of the modern Enlightenment values of reason and logic and science and data.* Not at all. Not at all. I'm all for the Enlightenment and reason and science and logic and rigor, absolutely. It's just that when I take reason seriously, it tells you its limits," he told me. "So if I respect logic, if I respect reason, then part of that respect is to respect that there are these absolute limits. Other than that, you're not really paying attention to what logic tells you and what reason says."

And what reason says, according to Hoffman, is some pretty incredible stuff. He expects eventually to build a falsifiable case for the idea that we all belong to a "universal oneness" that generates the reality we falsely believe to be real. But for now, he's confronting the fact that first he has to get people to see that they have been wrong about everything, at least since they started developing object permanence as infants.

"It's so radical to think that we don't see reality as it is, that this is all a virtual reality, because the implications of it go to the very core of who we believe we are," he told me. "There is no stopping this thing. If my body itself and my neurons and my brain are just a virtual-reality set of icons, then I have to rethink from the get-go who I am and what I am. The rot goes all the way down.

"So that's why I can understand why people get off this train. Because if you get on this train, there's nothing that you believe that survives. You have to completely rethink everything from top to bottom. So I understand my colleagues not wanting to do that. I didn't want to do it. And by the way, I'm still emotionally coming to grips with it."

Intellectually, however, Hoffman was moving forward without any sign of doubt. The third time we talked, he told me that he and his collaborators were on the brink of "a spectacular breakthrough."

"If this is right," Hoffman told me, "physics will never be the same."

This was quite a claim for a person who is not, after all, even a physicist. But being a cognitive scientist hasn't stopped him from rejecting the existence of the brain, and it hasn't stopped him, either, from venturing into the distant (and bizarre) frontier of modern physics, where reality is not the smoothly mechanistic machine it appears to be, where the physical world seems to a projection of some deeper structure.

For decades, Hoffman has followed along from afar as quantum physicists like Wheeler have probed deeper into the fundamental nature of Einstein's relativistic universe, zooming in on life at unfathomable proximities and unexpectedly discovering unstable and subjective forces at play.

They have found, for example, that electrons located far apart can appear so entangled as to be essentially undifferentiated, and that observation itself seems to alter physical reality. They have even found evidence that the three-dimensional world "is a hologram," as Stanford professor Leonard Susskind has written—that it is "an image of reality coded on a distant two-dimensional surface."

These discoveries, among others, point to a crack in spacetime's facade, to a fundamental limitation of the presumption that a coherent and consistent reality exists, that time and space are the fundamental dimensions of the universe. And this has led a prestigious sliver of physicists—Nima Arkani-Hamed, of the Institute for Advanced Study, among them—to explore theories of reality beyond spacetime, to posit that something must exist beneath the fabric of our reality, undergirding or projecting it.

It was a twenty-seven-part lecture that Arkani-Hamed gave at Harvard in 2019, in fact, that was the catalyst for Hoffman's new breakthrough. Watching it on YouTube, Hoffman recognized that he and Arkani-Hamed were trying to do the same thing: "to really go beyond spacetime in a fundamental way," Hoffman told me.

They were going toward the same place, to something more fundamental than matter, Hoffman believed. But they were approaching this invisible place from opposite directions. While Arkani-Hamed was working backward from the physical world to begin mapping what might underlie it, Hoffman was working forward toward the physical from the consciousness he believes exists "beneath" time and space, projecting the illusion of a material world.

"I realized this is it," Hoffman said. "They have found these structures beyond spacetime, and this is my chance to connect."

So he sat down and began transcribing Arkani-Hamed's lectures, "hour after hour." He got through fifteen of the twenty-seven, producing 586 single-spaced pages packed with daunting equations and bewildering diagrams, before he was hit, in early 2020, with a suspected case of COVID that brought him to the brink of death in a hospital bed, and to saying goodbye to his wife by text.

The breakthrough, he told me, was that he'd found a way to connect. He and his collaborators had discovered, they believed, mathematical evidence that directly linked the dynamics of consciousness to the structures Arkani-Hamed had described. Hoffman and his collaborators had, in other words, begun to model how mind creates what looks like reality.

It was hard to believe what I was hearing: a revelation that, if correct, would reorient everything to a degree that would make the Copernican revolution look like a failed coup, like a mere reordering of our position in a universe or, rather, in a mirage projected by a universal mind that no one had known existed, much less been able to describe, until now.

"I can even tell you what 'mass' means in terms of properties of conscious agents," he told me. "The whole thing is breaking open."

I wanted to hear more, but reality—whatever that meant anymore—was intruding. My son would wake up from his nap soon, and I would have to change his diaper and offer him food and pour him milk and find some way of occupying him. I was there physically, but already I was somewhere in the future, thinking about what it would be like to meet Hoffman in what he wouldn't call real life.

### IV.

Donald Hoffman may be a cognitive scientist who believes he doesn't have a brain or a face or a body, but when, one Monday morning last October, I entered his humble lab on the UC Irvine campus, there he was: a rangy man in an unbuttoned black polo shirt, khaki hiking pants, and a surgical mask.

He soon produced what appeared to me to be a dry-erase marker, began writing on what appeared to be a whiteboard, and enthusiastically picked up where we'd left off in our last Zoom meeting, optimistically explaining the rationale behind the breakthrough he'd just made.

"Did you get the idea of the decorated permutation?" he asked me. "Or I could put it on the board and explain it if you want."

Hoffman lost me for the next twelve minutes, as he made an earnest but doomed attempt to explain math to me. Afterward, I did my best to find my way to firm ground. Where our conversation went instead was somewhere almost mystical, to a discussion of what Hoffman thinks math means: that there's a universal mind of some kind, that it exists someplace outside time and space, and that we are it.

"Whatever the universe is beyond spacetime is unbounded intelligence, unbounded truths," Hoffman said.

Hoffman was refreshingly—inspiringly—willing to go wherever his radical argument led.

"To be consistent, I have to raise these hard questions, to confront my whole framework," he told me. "It's only as you try to confront these things—the deep questions—that you can then try to see the limitations in your own framework.

"And there is another way of looking at it, and that is that what happens in the headset is just what happens in the headset. So I put on a VR headset and I play *Grand Theft Auto*, and I'm playing with my friend Joe and I ram his Porsche over a cliff and he goes sailing off the cliff and crashes, and he and his Porsche disappear and then we remove our headsets and laugh and go have a Coke.

"In some sense, what happens inside spacetime isn't that serious. And that's again counterintuitive, because we think of spacetime as fundamental and so death is the end and there's nothing beyond and so life is very, very serious and you need to do whatever you can in your seventy years, whatever you might have, to try to get whatever recognition—the best writer, the best dancer, the best whatever it might be—or just have a good time, be the best partier, whatever it might be, because life is short. And you put all your eggs in that basket.

"But there's this other point of view that says, *You know what, it's just a headset. If you crash and burn, well, you just take your headset off. And what you learned in the process is what you learned.*

"So then the question is: *What am I? Who am I?* And the physicalist answer is: *Well, you're just a little package of particles. You're a piece of meat inside space and time. And when that package of meat dies, you and all your consciousness go with it.*

"Well, but spacetime isn't fundamental. That whole story just doesn't hold water. So I switched around from thinking, I'm just meat that has some consciousness associated with it, to saying, No, that assumes spacetime is fundamental; that violates our best science, so that's not right. And, best I can understand is, I'm not separate from that unbounded intelligence. Hoffman is just an avatar in spacetime of this unbounded intelligence. I'm just a projection of it. And so are you.

"So from this point of view, Don and Ted are just avatars of the one unbounded intelligence. And this unbounded intelligence is doing something that I'm very interested in understanding."

When he left the room to take a break, I peeked behind the curtains that occupied one of the lab's long walls. Instead of windows, I found that the curtains were covering mirrors because, Hoffman explained later, the lab had been used to observe the unwitting child subjects of psychology experiments before he took over the space. I couldn't follow the math or the physics at the heart of Hoffman's thinking, but standing before the reflective side of the one-way glass, I was starting to understand more of what he meant: that when we're looking out at the world, we're actually looking inward; that the state of our consciousness really is determinative of what we perceive; that we might be able to decode the significance seeping into everything if we were willing to remind ourselves anew that reality is inherently strange.

But while these insights were beginning to cohere as I looked in the mirror, it was the most obvious thing in the reflection that I still couldn't decipher: myself. Hoffman had upended my idea about what reality was and about how to understand what I perceived. But when I tried to apply his methodology to myself, I saw someone who might have been learning theories about reality that were entirely new but who felt exactly the same, who wore the same collared shirt he'd worn on his first Zoom interview with Hoffman, who wore fashionable glasses bought from a discount online retailer, who was willfully eccentric, embarrassingly pretentious, and cripplingly self-serious.

I'd traveled 1,200 miles from home in search of a truth I didn't yet know. And I'd found it. I was convinced that Hoffman was actually right, that life shouldn't be taken literally, that something far more

**I WAS STARTING TO UNDERSTAND MORE OF WHAT HE MEANT: THAT WHEN WE'RE LOOKING OUT AT THE WORLD, WE'RE ACTUALLY LOOKING INWARD; THAT THE STATE OF OUR CONSCIOUSNESS REALLY IS DETERMINATIVE OF WHAT WE PERCEIVE.**

mysterious and meaningful underlies it all, that worldly ambition is ridiculous, that the only thing worth achieving is an understanding that everything—including who we appear to be—is one nonphysical thing. But knowing rarely helps anything.

### V.

Hoffman of all people seemed to understand this. Even he has struggled, since he first detected a separation between perception and reality, in 1986, to acclimate to the implications of his ideas. In his mid-forties, Hoffman sought out psychiatric treatment and medication for his anxiety.

These days he prefers meditation. A lot of meditation—over thirty thousand hours, he estimates, over the last twenty years. Even so, on the brink of a breakthrough, his self-doubt sometimes wins out.

"My emotions rebel all the time," he told me. "There's a part of me that just doesn't believe this one bit. But now I realize, even now, consciously, just in the last few months, What if I am this unbounded intelligence and that is the source of all scientific ideas? What if I have a scientific problem and I say to myself: I would like to understand this problem. And then I go and let go of it altogether—I just literally let go

of all conceptions. If I really am that unbounded intelligence, maybe something amazing can happen."

This seemed like the terminus of Hoffman's inquiry, the bottom of the rabbit hole he'd brought me down. But this act of letting go was also, I realized, the origin of all Hoffman's thinking. It's easy, at least for me, to think of scientists as being bound to strict conventions, to unimpeachable rules of rationality. Hoffman, however, reminded me that it's scientists who are not simply inclined but actually required to suspend their beliefs. At least this is how Hoffman radically practices his profession.

"The fact is, I have no beliefs," Hoffman told me. "If I have any belief, it's that I don't believe any of my theories. I don't believe they're right, and I don't believe they're wrong. All I believe is that that's where our science is at right now, and so I'm just looking at what the mathematical structure of our science is right now. My beliefs are irrelevant."

And as he goes to increasingly unlikely places at the direction of his discoveries, Hoffman knows that even our most accurate possible description of reality can only gesture toward the full truth of what's actually happening. Invoking what are known as Gödel's incompleteness theorems, which seem to show that no mathematical theory can provide a theory of everything, Hoffman argues that the "truth transcends any formal theory that we could possibly come up with, infinitely," and that "there's an infinite realm of truths to be explored.

"That means that my theory itself is not even scratching the surface of the truth," he told me. But he doesn't think that means he shouldn't try. "It's not pointless to be trying to come up with theories, as long as you don't mistake what you're doing for the ultimate truth—if you just, I guess, view what you're doing as a useful perspective on reality, but just a perspective."

We had been talking in his lab for more than two hours by this point, and Hoffman was exhausted. He'd survived COVID, but he had not entirely recovered. He could work only a few hours a day now, and we were pushing his limit. He excused himself to take some heart medication, and when

he returned, he wanted to continue our conversation but needed a break from explaining himself.

"So maybe to let you talk for a minute," he said. "Why did you find this stuff interesting?"

This was the question I'd been asking myself the whole time without having come up with an answer, though now I decided to give it a try.

"I was just at the library one day, with my kids," I said. "And the title, it resonated. I wasn't having a good day, I guess. I wasn't enjoying reality."

Hoffman laughed, and I continued to grasp for an explanation.

"So I read it," I said, "and it weirdly made sense to me. I have always had this intuition that something is missing, that we're not seeing this right. Essentially, reality feels allegorical to me. It feels meaningful. And when you consider the time span of history"—the universe being almost fourteen billion years old and all that—"it has literally all been leading up to this moment. So it *is* meaningful."

But, I said, the explanations I'd been presented with—namely, Jesus and the Big Bang—weren't convincing. What his theory offered, I told Hoffman, was a way to think of reality as being not random, as science makes you assume, or heading toward some single revelation, as the Catholicism of my upbringing argued. Instead, it was like a fiction: a place where the furniture of the external world—the people and places and things—exists on a mental, not a physical, level, and where what happens matters, where everything is laden with metaphorical or thematic significance. Otherwise, it wouldn't be included.

"So I thought that was interesting," I told Hoffman—"the idea that what's real is not literal. It's symbolic."

And it wasn't just the theory, I explained, that compelled me. It was also the rigor, I said, with which his argument had been made.

"I'm no scientist or mathematician," I said, "but I was raised in a very logical framework. My dad's an economist. My mom's an epidemiologist." I had been raised, I explained, to think it was absurd to believe something you can't prove. My dad is a practicing Catholic, but his view of God, it seems to me, is not of some mystical truth, but of a slightly embarrassing but ultimately ennobling faith that allows one to more easily adopt positive human traits like compassion and patience and prudence. My mom, the daughter of Jewish refugees from Russia and Poland, had long adopted an avowed atheism, which she began to question only very recently, when she literally started reading *Judaism for Dummies*. I had recently done something similar: picked up at a used-books store an introduction to Zen Buddhism, in which I had read a description of the self as being like a flame: a process that operates within and upon its environment, not a discrete thing. I tried to tell Hoffman, in my garbled way, that his theory described something similar.

"It's a formal way of thinking about how we aren't these hermetically sealed things in a reality," I said, sounding stoned. "It's more complicated than that. There's a porousness or a connection between things. But as soon as you say that, it sounds so, I don't know, flighty. Kumbaya-ish, inherently. But your thinking is obviously not like that."

I talked more—probably too much—about my childhood. I brought up what he'd said about how we're inclined to view life as a mad dash to prove ourselves before we die. "That point was emphasized to me very, very much as a kid," I said. "'You only live once' was always sort of the mantra. And that creates a lot of anxiety or fear."

"And God's pissed if you do anything wrong," Hoffman said.

"What's interesting about your theory," I said, "is that it had a spiritual effect on me without having any spirituality in it."

## VI.

Soon after I stopped talking, we left the bizarre modernist building that held the windowless lab and went out for lunch in an outdoor mall across the street from campus, in what has been called the largest master-planned city in North America. On the patio of a chain health food restaurant, I ate brown rice and salmon with Hoffman, who, by this point in our relationship, I was calling Don. I was reluctant to let him go, so after we ate, I followed Don home, to a bland faculty housing development on the far side of campus, to the modest duplex with stucco siding where he's lived with his wife since 1987.

When we stopped outside, Don kept going, expounding on the differences between philosophy and science and excitedly discussing the possibility that light, which has no mass, could be a projection of conscious agents that have no connections. Then it was

time for him to leave me, and there I was, left on the corner of two dead-end streets, Schubert Court and Russell Court.

But I still wanted to follow him, even though he wasn't there, so I took a Lyft to Laguna Beach, to a state park he had recommended. Then I did something I had started doing only since I'd found his book, something I'd never done in public, something that embarrassed me: I sat on a rock that had been revealed by the tide, on the brink of the ocean, on the farthest edge of firm ground, and I meditated. I mean, I tried to meditate. I couldn't escape my thoughts. My consciousness had been overtaken by self-consciousness long ago, and so I couldn't even get to the starting line: to a willingness to be a fool, to make a case for what no one else sees. But at least I knew it was there. Or at least I thought I could see it, ahead in the distance.

Then I kept going. From the beach, I took a Lyft ride in a Tesla to a Thai restaurant in a strip mall. From there, I walked the rest of the way to the office-park hotel where I was staying because it had been the cheapest result on Kayak. On the way, I passed oblong shrubs and symmetrical plantings of palm trees. I crossed an empty campus of angular mid-rises that looked as dated as they did futuristic, and of deactivated water features. I came upon a traffic triangle with triangular trees planted on the periphery, hiding a triangular reflecting pool that occupied the center. The setting seemed clearly symbolic, but I wasn't sure what it symbolized. That things were starting to take a new shape? That my thinking was becoming more angular?

More rigid, perhaps? Or maybe more precise?

I had come to Hoffman with some hope that he would have answers that solved the riddles of reality: Who are we? Where are we? And what are we in the world for? But even he knew on some level that the truth is ultimately elusive. What mattered was that he'd made them into riddles again. He'd done what I'd always wanted to do with my own writing without knowing it until now: turned the supposedly predictable, mechanistic universe into a koan again, into a paradox that might provoke insight. For, as he'd told me, "we seem to be in a universe in which, even though the truth completely transcends anything that could be described, here we are trying to describe it."

When I reached my hotel, I took an elevator to my room, looked out the filthy windows of the high-rise, and marveled at the odd geometry of this real-life *SimCity*, at a sunset that looked like a screen saver. Or at least that's how it appeared to me. ★

---

# ALGAE

## KELP

*by Jennifer Kabat*

**FEATURES:**

★ Between five and twenty-five million years old
★ Carbon-negative
★ Makes clouds

Picture George Eliot: long face, long nose, dressed as a man. She and her common-law husband, George Lewes, are both in "a wide-awake hat" and "an old coat, with manifold pockets in unexpected places, over which is slung a leathern case, containing hammer, chisel…" They also each wield two knives, and wear "trousers warranted not to spoil." It is the summer of 1856, on the craggy Devon coast, and Eliot has recently adopted Lewes's surname. Together, they haunt tide pools, and Eliot discovers the "difference… between having eyes and seeing." They "scramble," she writes, over a shoreline that is "nothing but huge boulders and jutting rocks." Here, she falls in love. "Quite in love," she puts it, "with seaweeds." She adds, "I shall never forget their appearance… the dark olive fronds of the Laminariae."

Me too, with the same seaweed: *Laminaria digitata*—kelp.

I come to it after an apocalyptic email warns me to eat seaweed. The missive invokes the war in Ukraine and threats to its nuclear reactors. *The New York Times* reports that Russian troops have dug trenches in Chernobyl's radioactive dirt, sending Geiger counters clicking madly. Kelp is the most iodine-rich food in the world, so hopefully protection.

I start eating more seaweed, much more, and begin to spend hours, days, avoiding writing, googling seaweed, following every seaweed-fact rabbit hole. *Kelp* is a vague name for certain brown seaweeds, I learn. Seaweeds themselves are macroalgae, and there are three kinds: red, green, and brown. Red and green seaweeds are plants and brown is a chromist. Red and green represent the oldest forms of plant life: green seaweed 1 billion years old; red even older, 1.6 billion years. Kelp has been around for between five and twenty-five million years. Not vascular plants, these macroalgae are permeable to their environment, allowing them to absorb nutrients at a rate higher than those of terrestrial plants. There are thirty types of laminaria alone, and some grow more than a foot a day. The *Laminaria digitata* has blades like fingers—that is, if fingers were slick, brown, and leathery.

There is talk that giant kelp forests could halt climate change, because seaweed is carbon-negative, and kelp grows so quickly. It can clean heavy metals and nuclear waste from ocean water, and there are heady reports of seaweed-based bioplastics and biofuels. Not to mention the litany of ailments kelp might cure: HIV, HPV, cancer (colon and breast). It is anti-tumor, anti-obesity, and fights diabetes (goodbye, Ozempic). It's antimicrobial, so no more antibiotics (or antibiotic resistance) and might even cure COVID, thanks to the iodine it contains.

All the scientific studies are driven by breaking kelp into singular elements, things to extract to fix ourselves and our world, rather than seeing how its constituent parts work together in one organism—and the sheer awe that understanding can produce.

None of this research existed in Eliot's time. All she had there on the rocks was the looking, the wonder, and the love, her eyes opened. That summer she is still Mary Ann Evans, not yet Eliot, and, dressed as a man as she searches the shore, she's free. My favorite thing about laminaria—it makes clouds. When exposed to the sun and waves at low tide, kelp releases iodide to reduce the stress, and this iodide seeds clouds. I see Eliot bathed in kelp-clouds, her own stress released, and I imagine this is what frees her, during these months in Devon, to begin writing fiction. I am sure there are long walks, and talks about this with Lewes. The two share everything, and as a novelist she becomes George Eliot, taking his first name in her professional life, as she has taken his last name in her personal one. But just as I have turned to seaweed in my anxiety and procrastination, I picture her in the clouds, and as she searches for seaweed, she, too, is released from whatever fears she's had. This vision makes me love seaweed the most: these cloud-creating algae helping Eliot write her novels. ★

*Illustration by Madison Ketcham*

# JIM JARMUSCH

[FILMMAKER, MUSICIAN]

"MY FAVORITE THING IS TO WAKE UP AND HAVE NO PLAN."

Some of the music Jim Jarmusch would play for aliens, if they came to visit Earth:
*Muddy Waters*
*Gustav Mahler's Ninth Symphony*
*Indian classical music*
*A Merle Haggard song*

**J**im Jarmusch is best known as an American filmmaker, with titles such as the Caméra d'Or winner Stranger Than Paradise, Down by Law, Broken Flowers, and Mystery Train *establishing him as a cinematic force with a penchant for high drama and deadpan humor. Born in Cuyahoga Falls, Ohio, Jarmusch came to New York to study literature and film. While filmmaking is a passion, Jarmusch has a deep curiosity and a seemingly inexhaustible well of creativity that cannot be contained by one medium. He is also a screenwriter, a poet, a collage artist, and, as will become clear in our conversation, a voracious reader and beaver enthusiast. His musical endeavors with his band, SQÜRL, have been taking up much of his time lately.*

*Jarmusch and producer and musician Carter Logan formed SQÜRL in 2009 to score Jarmusch's film The Limits of Control. They favor heavy percussion, analog synths, and distorted guitars layered into ambient textures, effecting a dreamy,*

*Illustration by Kristian Hammerstad*

*hypnotic atmosphere that, aptly, feels cinematic. After creating music together for over a decade, including numerous EPs and film scores, SQÜRL has now released its first full-length record, Silver Haze. The album was produced by Randall Dunn, who has worked with heavy ambient and boundary-pushing acts including Sunn O))) and Zola Jesus. To add another layer to their wall of sound, the band brought in actor-singer Charlotte Gainsbourg, singer-poet Anika, and guitarist Marc Ribot as collaborators. The result is a mesmerizing album that is understated and moody, an immersive experience that feels like a trip into another world. It's challenging and rewarding, an effect not dissimilar to that of watching one of Jarmusch's movies.*
—*Melissa Locker*

## I. GYM SOCKS AND WEED

THE BELIEVER: When I interviewed you back in 2014 for *The Guardian*, you said you were going to put out an album "eventually." So it's now 2023. I guess "eventually" is nine years?

JIM JARMUSCH: [*Laughing*] Yeah, I guess so. People keep asking, "Why an album, now?" We don't have an answer. We don't have a master plan. And we do other things. We have other projects. Carter plays in another excellent band called Leathered. I do musical projects with other people. And, of course, we do film things. Also, I find it kind of funny—or interesting, maybe—how the format of these things is arbitrary. Well, not arbitrary. A feature film is ninety minutes to two and a half hours, because that's the turnover in the theaters for making a profit, right? Why are albums a certain number of songs? That's what would fit on a vinyl record. Why is the single a certain length? It's for radio play. So all these things to me are kind of ridiculous, especially now, when you can release a film of any length, streaming-wise. Or you can release music of any length. Personally, I love an EP because I like the length of them and I like making them, too, because it's a little more control. But anyway, we were ready to make an album. We had a lot of material, we had been talking with [producer] Randall Dunn, who we love and who's worked with a lot of people we are inspired by, so it just sort of happened. So we did the album…

BLVR: When we spoke before, you said you love EPs, so I was a little surprised about a full-length.

JJ: Yeah, I was a little surprised too! But it was fun to do. We had enough stuff where we could have done a whole album of songs with vocals, or we could have done a whole album of instrumental things, or we could have done a whole album with guests reciting texts over musical landscapes that we'd created. We just worked with Randall and played him a lot of stuff we had, and he helped us navigate toward this thing called an album.

BLVR: Since you have so many songs, do you feel like you are going to do more albums?

JJ: I don't know: maybe. But it may be, you know, fifteen years. [*Laughs*] There may be some EPs in between. I hope. I still love that format.

But, you know, we're not twenty years old, and we're not going to conquer the world with our rock-and-roll band. That's just not the case. We are artists doing different things, and our music is important to us, and we spend a lot of time doing it. We've done scores for films. Carter and I just did a kind of exhausting tour of Europe where we played our live scores to the surrealist films of Man Ray from one hundred years ago. We've been involved in those films being restored, and they will hopefully be released with our score at some point. So we take the music seriously. We work at it, but we do other things too.

BLVR: Because you are both artists, and not totally beholden to the structures of a classic album, did you consider doing a double album or a massive box set or something?

JJ: We kind of deferred to Randall on that one. We sort of treated him like our navigator, because we really trust him, and he was kind of our guide in shaping these things. But we played him a lot of music, and then he helped us focus down to this silver haze.

BLVR: Randall Dunn worked with Sunn O))), who you referenced as an inspiration.

JJ: Yes, he did.

BLVR: I saw them at Le Guess Who? festival in Utrecht, in

the Netherlands, and that is the loudest concert I have ever been to in my life.

JJ: I have special earplugs that reduce the decibels rather than dampening the music, which I acquired only after maybe the third time seeing them. Swans are pretty fucking loud too. I don't know if you've ever seen them live.

BLVR: I haven't, but I have been in the front row of a Slayer concert, and I low-key thought I was gonna die.

JJ: I saw Slayer once at Irving Plaza [in New York City] many years ago, and the entire ground floor was the mosh pit. It was wild.

BLVR: Congratulations on surviving that!

JJ: It was crazy. I was with my girlfriend. And I took her there as a surprise without telling her what band we were going to see. And then she said, "Oh my god, we better go on the balcony. This is terrifying." We went upstairs, and she was one of the very few females in the whole place too. It was kind of strange.

BLVR: I have been at shows like that at Irving Plaza.

JJ: The whole place smells like gym socks or something.

BLVR: I believe that's gym socks and weed. I feel like this is sort of a loaded term, but is this a concept album?

JJ: Not to my knowledge. I'm not quite sure what the concept would be.

BLVR: I asked because the press materials for the album came with a very long list of things that you like and dislike, including things like insects and animals and oscillation.

JJ: Yeah, we just tried to put together a list of things rather than just do the traditional *Jim and Carter met while creating music for a film, blah, blah, blah*. Of course, in the end, I think they gave you something like that too. We just wanted something a little less formulaic for people to read. Some sort of random thoughts about our inspirations in general. We're

not really interested in explaining things. We don't really analyze ourselves. I have that a lot with my films too. People ask me what things mean, and I have no idea! When you make a film, it's like two years later that people are asking you about it, and you're not even the same person. It's sort of the same with a record. It's hard for me, in particular, to talk about things I created, because I'm not analytical. I need to protect a kind of mystery for myself.

## II. PLATO'S CAVE

BLVR: I read an interview where you said it was hard for you to appreciate your own films because of the process of creating them and the time lag before they're released. Do you feel the same way about your music?

JJ: In a way, but a bit less for several reasons. One, I'm very involved in the music and in its creation, but I'm collaborating on a little more of a basic level with other people. In a film, I'm collaborating with a lot of people to realize it, but I'm sort of the captain of the ship, because I wrote it, I cast it, I will be in the editing room. But I can never see it again for the first time. That's impossible because of how it's created. The beauty of films is they are like a dream that you enter, and unless you've seen it before, you don't know where it's taking you. Music is similar, although music is less dependent on an image or a narrative, so it's even more abstract and beautiful in a way. But it doesn't take as long to create. That's a difference. I'm sorry; I'm not being very articulate. There's a difference and a similarity and I'm not making them very clear. They're not very clear to me, I guess.

BLVR: I found the quote that I was referring to. You said, "The beauty of cinema is that you're basically walking into Plato's Cave." I really have to applaud you on just casually dropping Plato's Cave into the conversation.

JJ: [*Laughs*] Right. Plato's Cave: they're just projecting shadows on a wall. And really, if aliens came down from another world, they would think, Wow, you spend all this time with this equipment, these machines, to capture and imitate reality, and then you bring people into a dark cave and show them these images projected, which are sort of imitating what's just outside the cave. [*Cracking up*] It's a ridiculous thing, if you look at it from a kind of overview.

But, I don't know, I love making films and watching them, and I love making music.

BLVR: So if aliens came down to Earth—after they finished judging the existence of filmmaking—what kind of music would you want to play for them? Do you think SQÜRL or Sunn O))) would be a great option for them?

JJ: Oh gosh. Well, I'd certainly play Bach to them immediately, because the repetition and variation are such beautiful things. As for rock and roll, I don't know. I'd probably play some blues: Robert Johnson or maybe Muddy Waters. I'd play them some sort of avant-garde or more experimental jazz, maybe Ornette Coleman. I'd want to play them something, you know, orchestral: maybe Gustav Mahler's Ninth Symphony or something like that. And then I would try to play them some country songs or pop songs. Maybe some African or Ethiopian music, and then a Merle Haggard song or something. I would want to show them how we have this diversity of music on the planet that is so beautiful—maybe some Indian classical music and sitar to see how they reacted to those vibrations, you know. That would be a fun project! Send them to my house if you encounter them.

BLVR: I would go full Eurovision, just as a great symbol of all people coming together.

JJ: Um, yeah. Send them to my house, although I remember William Burroughs saying something like [*slips into William Burroughs's voice*] "We have no reason to believe these aliens would be benevolent in any way." Who knows. I'd be wary.

BLVR: That was an excellent William Burroughs impression!

JJ: Thank you. I worked on a really good film, a documentary called *Burroughs*, made by Howard Brookner, and he and I were the two-man crew for quite a long time, just hanging out with Burroughs in the late '70s. If you want to watch that film, it's on Criterion.

BLVR: Do you ever find you're on an airplane, thinking, You know, I haven't caught up on all the *Twilight* films? Do you watch mass-market movies, or do you tend to only watch obscure Indian dramas?

JJ: No, I'm not hierarchical. I have my preferences, but because I really, deeply love the craft of filmmaking, I, of course, like masterful filmmakers' work. But I watch all kinds of stuff. On a plane recently I watched *Cruella*. I love the *Naked Gun* movies because they're so stupid. I'm sort of amazed by the *John Wick* movies, just by how many people he can kill. I haven't seen the *Twilight* movies. And I have particular things I will never see. I will never see any *Star Wars* films, because I resent that I know so much about them and the characters. Why is all that in my head when I've never actually seen one, you know? Why do I know about R2-D2 and Darth Vader and all these things when I've never even seen any *Star Wars* film? I've never seen *Gone with the Wind* and I never will, just because I feel like it's forced on me and it's some kind of corny thing.

But these are very subjective, just kind of stubborn things on my part. I don't like mass things being shoved on me, but I will go see them. Like *The Terminator* is a masterpiece of cinema. It's a big action movie, essentially. So I don't really differentiate. But I have to tell you one thing I hate—and you can just do a little test yourself: watch any recent action-oriented movie and look for any shot that's more than three seconds long. I find that really insulting and shit filmmaking: like they have to keep it moving every three seconds. And that's the longest they'll leave a shot on! And then cut. One second, cut! Two seconds, cut! Three seconds, cut! Man, I get a headache. I just turn it off. I'm like, *Come on, man, go to film school! Watch something! Go read a book! Look at a painting! Look at something. This is nonsense.* I can't stand that.

BLVR: Guess they should go watch *Birdman* to get inspired.

JJ: Yeah, or just watch something that's not a formula like that.

BLVR: Well, the only thing you need to watch in the *Twilight* movies is the clip where the vampires are playing baseball. You can google it. Truly a masterpiece.

One of the things that popped out to me in your SQÜRL press materials was that you thought a lot of visual artists were musical, and musical artists were visual. And I wanted to sort of explore that with you, because you mentioned my great uncle Mark Rothko, who's not known for his musical taste, so I was intrigued.

JJ: I believe in this kind of aesthetic synesthesia, where certain things suggest something else to your senses. Rothko's a great example because his work is meditative. You can go into another place under the influence of a visual thing like that. And of course, there's the beautiful piece of music "Rothko Chapel" that Morton Feldman created, inspired by the paintings or the feeling of them or that kind of meditative place you could go. So we put that in there because we love when certain things suggest another form like that. Or you smell something and you think of a color. It really speaks to me when the work of painters or musicians suggests another form. I don't know how to explain it any more than the openness of that kind of synesthesia.

### III. THE HOSPITALITY OF BEAVERS

BLVR: In addition to filmmaking and music, you make collages. Are there more creative outlets that you have?

JJ: Yeah, I write poems. For a long time, I studied with Kenneth Koch. The New York School of Poets are kind of my godfathers throughout everything I make—movies as well. That's why I'm so happy we have these John Ashbery poems on *Silver Haze*. I'm preparing a new series of collages. I have one book of collages that I put out and I'm working on a new little book. It's not quite ready. I am going to have a show in Paris, and then I'm going to have a show of my collages next year in LA. They're all very small and sort of unassuming and very minimal. So yeah: films, music, collages. I write poems; I write essays, sort of; and sort-of prose poems. I do a lot of writing as well. Not like elaborate fiction projects. I'm not writing a novel or anything like that. But I love poems, too, because like in music, the spaces in between sort of accumulate into the overall thing. And my collages are very minimal. And they're about reappropriating images and reduction, and removing things and substituting things—very minor ways of altering your perception of the visual image. I like a lot of things. Not just art. I'm an amateur mycologist: I've been trying to learn mushroom identification for twenty years now. I observe birds and animals and try to learn about different types of moss, of which there

are so many varieties. For a while I just was obsessed with the history of motorcycle design, especially European and Japanese. I get sucked into tangents because I'm really a kind of dilettante. I don't consider that a negative thing. There're so many things that are interesting to me that I can't imagine not being kind of scatterbrained, in a way.

BLVR: Do you sleep?

JJ: I sleep! I sleep and then I wake up sort of vibrating. Like I'm reading this book called *Beaverland*, about the history of beavers in North America, their behavior—well, everything about them. It's incredible!

BLVR: That sounds incredible, but maybe a bad thing to google?

JJ: [*Laughs*] Well, yeah. I hope this isn't inappropriate, but beavers have two layers of fur. The outer layer is thick. The amount of hair on one square inch of a beaver is more than on a human head. So they have this layer of very thick fur that is waterproof and very warm. Underneath it they have an incredibly soft layer of fur, which is what people would use to make beaver hats. They used it for clothing and things. But it's also where the slang word *beaver* for females comes from: because of this incredible softness of beavers.

BLVR: Well, I'm from the Beaver State, so all beaver facts are a go for me.

JJ: OK, good. I thought that was a beautiful fact, that that feminine softness of the inner fur suggested that slang.

BLVR: And have you gotten to the part about beaver butts and vanilla yet?

JJ: No, I've just started reading about their castor glands.

BLVR: Well, spoiler, but that's where artificial vanilla scent can come from.

JJ: Yeah, I'm just starting that part. Man, that's so bizarre. Another cool thing about beavers is that in the winter, sometimes other animals will come into the beavers' dam, or home. And instead of the beavers considering them invaders, the beavers accept them as guests. When they go out to gather food for their beaver families, they even bring extra food to their guests. I mean, it's just so cool! They are just so busy and then they are thinking, Well, I'm working anyway. I might as well bring some home for the guests too. They're also very funny and they play games. I'm so fed up with human centrism, you know?

BLVR: I know! You mentioned that you are interested in mycology. Did you happen to watch *The Last of Us*?

JJ: *The Last of Us*? No.

BLVR: It's an HBO series. And it's not really a spoiler, because it's in the first three seconds, but a mushroom—or fungus, rather—takes over. And while it's not a particularly hopeful show, I was hopeful that it could get people out of themselves and start looking more closely at the natural world. Even if it's just at the potential that mushrooms can take over and kill us all.

JJ: Yeah, I'm gonna check it out. Mushrooms are very strange, because they're medicinal, and also they can be poisonous. They can be psychoactive or they can kill you or they can be delicious. They are very complicated.

### IV. THE SCORE IS BETTER THAN THE FILM

BLVR: We got sidetracked, but you said you do sleep occasionally, but wake up vibrating. Is that because you're so enthused? Do the beavers inspire you with their industriousness?

JJ: No, no, it was an example that I went to sleep and I was reading about beavers and then I woke up and was like, Oh my god, I gotta read some more about beavers right away! The book is fascinating to me. But I wake up usually thinking, Oh my god, there's music and there's books and there's things in the world I don't even know about yet. There's so many things I could learn about the natural world. I get sort of excited to have a consciousness sometimes. But, you know, sometimes I'm just depressed because I have to do my laundry and stuff like everybody else.

BLVR: Laundry is depressing. When you are inspired to create and have so many creative outlets to choose from, how do you direct that energy?

JJ: I often have things I have to focus on because they involve other people, like if I am scheduled to work on a certain thing. My favorite thing of all is to wake up, especially where I am now, upstate, where I have my little recording studio, my art room, my place I create and write and whatever. My favorite thing is to wake up and have no plan. If I have no plan for the day, I'm in ecstasy and I become very productive just because I know there is nothing I have to do. Neil Young once said to me, "You know, the best plan is no plan." I agree with that one.

BLVR: So was the pandemic lockdown a really inspiring time for you? Did it change your life much?

JJ: It was kind of great, because I made my book of collages. I laid down a lot of the tracks that became *Silver Haze*. I wrote two scripts, basically. I did a lot of work. I also watched about seven or eight films every week. I did a lot of things. I was kind of relieved to not have to do any social things. There was something really good about it in a way. But also, it was very moving. And all the social unrest and Black Lives Matter was very moving to me. I felt sort of hyperemotional during that period, because everything was so strange. The world kind of just stopped. I got a lot done because I didn't have a plan. Yeah, it was pretty good.

BLVR: Wow, that's great. Personally, I just rewatched all the *Twilight* movies and did a lot of emotional eating. Not to keep throwing your words back in your face, but your press materials said that SQÜRL sometimes likes "the score better than the film." I was thinking of *Judgment Night*, but were you thinking of anything in particular?

JJ: No, not really. This is not really answering that. But I get very annoyed by how music and film seem to be all, I don't know, cut from the same ream of cloth. The world has so much diversity of music, so why do these commercial films all sound the fucking same, you know? But that's sort of the opposite of what you're asking. I love the fact that some scores of recent films have come not from John Williams or other traditional Hollywood kinds of shit. People like Nick Cave and Warren Ellis have made some beautiful scores for films. Trent Reznor and Atticus what's-his-name [Ross] made some beautiful scores. I've watched a few films only because Nick and Warren scored them. Otherwise, I might not even have been attracted to them. The scores are very important and also sometimes extremely annoying. I don't like it when the score is designed to tell you how to feel about everything, which is often the case. I find it sort of condescending and insulting. As someone who loves how films are made, why does the music have to tell you how to feel? It seems kind of lame.

BLVR: How do you fight against that?

JJ: First of all, whoever's making the music, whether it's me or it's the RZA or Tom Waits, I don't give them specific places to score. I don't say, *Here are the cues, I want to score here, I want melancholy music here*. I don't do that. I talk about the atmosphere of the film and encourage them—or encourage myself, if I am doing it—to make music that is derived from the feeling of the film. Then we'll take it and play with it in the editing room and see where the film likes it. That alleviates a lot of that idea of trying to tell the audience what's going on or how they should feel. Instead, it's adding another landscape like painting in the sky. That, to me, makes the most beautiful music because it becomes part of the fabric of the film.

BLVR: There's this meme of sorts where people replace an iconic soundtrack or score with something totally different—like they take the end of *Dirty Dancing* and add the music from *The Muppet Show* and it just dramatically changes it.

JJ: Yeah, that stuff is really fun, because it shows you how a visual image will absorb the music or how your brain will connect them, even though they weren't connected initially. I remember, when I first moved to New York, there was a period where I was really interested in early jazz from the '20s and '30s. I used to love playing those records while looking out the window and smoking weed and watching how the world would think to the music. It was so much fun. I know it's a kind of stoner cliché, but it was really remarkable. And it's the same thing: you throw music on a moving image in an editing room, such divergent types of music, and then see how the image absorbs it. It's really amusing and fun, but kind of fascinating, too, because it involves your brain accepting something, or making it connect things that weren't designed to connect somehow. I think it's a really kind of interesting exercise.

## V. A THEORY OF HUMAN EXPRESSION

BLVR: When I interviewed you back in 2014, you refused to explain the origins of the name SQÜRL. Have you changed your stance on that?

JJ: No. Because it's available to be deciphered very easily. So I'm not going to help people decipher.

BLVR: Ugh, fine, google.com it is.

JJ: Well, I don't know about google. But it's findable. It's kind of obvious. Once you find it, you'll think, Oh shit. You know, you'll think, Oh man, that guy. What the hell, that's too obvious.

BLVR: You once said, "Nothing is original. Steal from anywhere that resonates with inspiration." Hollywood really likes to reboot things. So if people started rebooting your movies, would you be OK with that?

JJ: What does that mean, "reboot"?

BLVR: Where they basically redo your entire film but update it with a new cast or some other twist. Like if they redid *Stranger Than Paradise* with the *High School Musical* cast.

JJ: Oh yeah, I think that'd be very amusing. I have to clarify what I mean by "stealing." I don't condone, like, if my neighbor wrote a script and I read it and then I took his script and made a film out of it before he could. However, in my case, that's not really a problem. If someone stole my script, they wouldn't make the same thing *I* would make, you know? At the same time, it's not cool to take something someone hasn't realized. But if anything in the world has been realized already, I don't see why it can't be sampled or imitated. I don't understand why that should be prevented. If you steal a riff from somebody and then make that the opening of "Stairway to Heaven," which Led Zeppelin did. Led Zeppelin is a great band, but they just blatantly stole blues songs and then said they wrote them. That's just kind of bullshit. You should credit the things you steal from. You should rejoice in them! You should say, *I was inspired by this.* You shouldn't say, *No, that came from me. I did that all myself.* Right? That's kind of bullshit. But I think all human expression is like waves in the ocean. And if you sample something in a hip-hop song, you're taking it somewhere else; you're using it as an element in something you're making now. Nothing's really original. There are only a small number of stories you can tell. There's just an infinite number of ways to tell that story. So it's not cool to take something someone else did verbatim and say you did it. That's just lame, but anything should be free to be inspiration.

BLVR: So no copyrighting a groove?

JJ: I don't know about copyrighting; it's all very complicated. I'm really interested in reappropriation, meaning you take something from somewhere else and make it something else. That's the basis of all art. Bach taught us that by his *Variations.* He just started varying things. And then it's like unfolding a beautiful Fibonacci code of everything. It's something ingrained in expression. John Lennon said something really cool. I don't have the exact quote. But he said something like: originality comes from not quite being able to imitate your greatest inspirations. I think that's a beautiful way of saying what I was trying to say. Like when Quentin Tarantino made his first film, *Reservoir Dogs,* he lifted the plot from a Hong Kong movie by director Ringo Lam called *City on Fire.* So I saw the film back then and I was like, Wow, he lifted that whole cloth and made it his own. That's really cool, but is he going to tell us that? And he did… eventually. And Quentin is all about inspiration from other places. So I'm all for that. Is that stealing? No: he reappropriated something and made it into something else by using very basic elements of somebody else's idea. That's the basis for all kinds of creation. How many paintings in the Renaissance are there of the Madonna and Child? Does that mean somebody stole the image? Also, for me, variation and repetition are really the most beautiful things in art

history, and the creation of things. Look at Rothko's paintings: they're variations of themselves in a way. He is like Bach to me. He can continue making these variations, and each one resonates in its own way.

BLVR: Rothko's favorite musician was Mozart, or at least that's what he mostly listened to.

JJ: Really interesting. I'm more of a Bach guy. Mozart is not my guy, although I greatly appreciate him. Did we talk at all about teenagers? Because they are the origins of new things in music and style and clothes and culture.

BLVR: And language.

JJ: In language! I look to teenagers, whether it's Rimbaud and Mary Shelley or Joan of Arc or Billie Eilish or whatever. The history of rock and roll comes out of teenagers, you know? So that's so important to me, but why am I talking about teenagers?

BLVR: Because they are so delightful?

JJ: Oh, because of Mozart! Because Mozart made a lot of that music when he was a teenager! So important.

BLVR: Well, thank you for taking the time to talk with me. Sorry if I spoiled *Beaverland.*

JJ: I'm also reading a great book called *Camera Man* [*: Buster Keaton, the Dawn of Cinema, and the Invention of the Twentieth Century*], a biography of Buster Keaton, one of my cinematic heroes. It's about him, but it's also about all the concurrent things happening through his life in the twentieth century. It's a really great book. So I'm alternating between them.

BLVR: Well, I guess that's where I'll leave you—between Buster Keaton and *Beaverland.*

JJ: Well, cool. Thanks for your mind and your thoughts and your consciousness. ✱

# THE STRANGE WORLD OF UNAUTHORIZED MOVIE REMAKES

# UNCANNY VIDEO

Unauthorized movie remakes often have odd origins—a sort of bootleg bizarro Hollywood where scripts are skeletal, actors are amateurish. special effects are neither special nor effective— and filmmakers' motivations are, at best, questionable. At the same time, creating unauthorized remakes is more than simple bootlegging. What do you need to bootleg? A printer? Some moxie? A blanket? A car with a trunk? It takes a whole other level of creative commitment to make an entirely new movie (even a psychedelically bad one). There is a sort of frightening joy in witnessing the ill-conceived (or ill-funded, or ill-executed) creative wagers of others. Unless you're working for Asylum Studios, making movies like *The Amazing Bulk* or *Transmorphers*—you literally are the worst.

*—Justin Cauler, with research by Eliza Browning and Emma-Li Downer*

## TANGENTIAL TRANSLATIONS

| | | |
|---|---|---|
| SEVEN SAMURAI (1954) | THE MAGNIFICENT SEVEN (1960) | |
| | SPIDER-MAN (1960?, TV) CAPTAIN AMERICA (1966?, TV) | THREE GIANT MEN (1973) |

Akira Kurosawa, whose films have often been remade, sued the studio that made *The Magnificent Seven*, and won.

Also known as *Captain America and Santo vs. Spider-Man*. Its popularity spawned many other Hollywood rip-offs.

| | | |
|---|---|---|
| THE EXORCIST (1973) | SEYTAN (1974) | |
| | STAR WARS (1978) | THE MAN WHO SAVED THE WORLD (1982) |

Incredibly, this film is a nearly shot-for-shot remake (that looks like it was shot on a camcorder).

Called "Turkish *Star Wars*" for its use of footage, music, and sound effects from *Star Wars* (and other sci-fi films).

| | |
|---|---|
| E.T. THE EXTRATERRESTRIAL (1982) | BADI (1984) |
| | MAD MAX: FURY ROAD (2015) MAD SHELIA: VIRGIN ROAD (2016) |

There's not a lot of information out there about this one. All that is apparent is that the friendly alien is horrifying.

*Virgin Road* is the first in a series, followed by *Revenge of the Road* (and possibly more).

## SURREPTITIOUS SEQUELS

| | | | |
|---|---|---|---|
| SPARTACUS (1960) | THE SLAVE (1962) | JAWS (1975) | JAWS 5: CRUEL JAWS (1995) |

Clocked as a sequel to *Spartacus* in part because it includes a character named Varinia, invented for Kubrick's film.

Also known as *The Beast, JS:CJ* is a direct-to-video Italian horror film shot in Florida.

| | | | |
|---|---|---|---|
| DAWN OF THE DEAD (1978) | ZOMBI 2 (1979) | TROLL (1986) | TROLL 2 (1990) |

*D.o.t.D* was released in Italy as *Zombi* (with a different cut and a new score). *Zombi 2* begins the Italian line of sequels.

Originally titled *Goblins* (and featuring goblins, not trolls), it was marketed as a sequel to *Troll* by the distributor.

| | | | |
|---|---|---|---|
| SHOWGIRLS (1995) | SHOWGIRLS 2: PENNY'S FROM HEAVEN (2010) | BORAT (2006) | MY BROTHER, BORAT (N/A) |

A Kickstarter-funded autofiction sequel written, produced, edited, and directed by *Showgirls* actor Rena Riffel.

Never released. *M.B.B.* was intended by the writer/director to address misconceptions of Kazakhstan as portrayed in *Borat*.

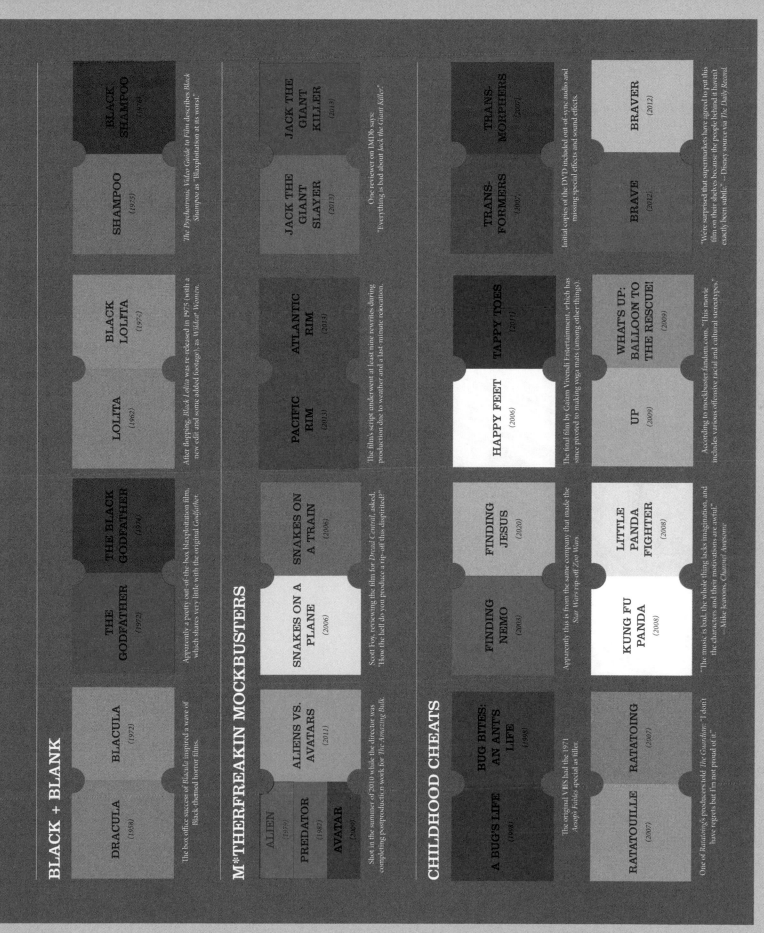

## BLACK + BLANK

DRACULA *(1958)* — BLACULA *(1972)*

The box office success of *Blacula* inspired a wave of Black-themed horror films.

THE GODFATHER *(1972)* — THE BLACK GODFATHER *(1974)*

Apparently a pretty out-of-the-box blaxploitation film, which shares very little with the original *Godfather*.

LOLITA *(1962)* — BLACK LOLITA *(1975)*

After flopping, *Black Lolita* was re-released in 1975 (with a new edit and some added footage), as *Wildcat Women*.

SHAMPOO *(1975)* — BLACK SHAMPOO *(1976)*

The *Psychotronic Video Guide to Film* describes *Black Shampoo* as "Blaxploitation at its worst."

## M*THERFREAKIN MOCKBUSTERS

ALIEN *(1979)* / PREDATOR *(1987)* / AVATAR *(2009)* — ALIENS VS. AVATARS *(2011)*

Shot in the summer of 2010 while the director was completing postproduction work for *The Amazing Bulk*.

SNAKES ON A PLANE *(2006)* — SNAKES ON A TRAIN *(2006)*

Scott Foy, reviewing the film for *Dread Central*, asked, "How the hell do you produce a rip-off of this dispirited?"

PACIFIC RIM *(2013)* — ATLANTIC RIM *(2013)*

The film's script underwent at least nine rewrites during production due to weather and a last-minute relocation.

JACK THE GIANT SLAYER *(2013)* — JACK THE GIANT KILLER *(2013)*

One reviewer on IMDb says: "Everything is bad about *Jack the Giant Killer*."

## CHILDHOOD CHEATS

A BUG'S LIFE *(1998)* — BUG BITES: AN ANT'S LIFE *(1998)*

The original VHS had the 1971 *Aesop's Fables* special as filler.

RATATOUILLE *(2007)* — RATATOING *(2007)*

One of *Ratatoing*'s producers told *The Guardian*: "I don't have regrets but I'm not proud of it."

FINDING NEMO *(2003)* — FINDING JESUS *(2020)*

Apparently this is from the same company that made the *Star Wars* rip-off *Zoo Wars*.

HAPPY FEET *(2006)* — TAPPY TOES *(2011)*

The final film by Gaiam Vivendi Entertainment, which has since pivoted to making yoga mats (among other things).

KUNG FU PANDA *(2008)* — LITTLE PANDA FIGHTER *(2008)*

"The music is bad, the whole thing lacks imagination, and the characters and their motivations are awful."
—Mike Ieavons, *Channel Awesome*

UP *(2009)* — WHAT'S UP: BALLOON TO THE RESCUE! *(2009)*

According to mockbuster.fandom.com, "This movie includes various offensive racial and cultural stereotypes."

TRANSFORMERS *(2007)* — TRANSMORPHERS *(2007)*

Initial copies of the DVD included out of sync audio and missing special effects and sound effects.

BRAVE *(2012)* — BRAVER *(2012)*

"We're surprised that supermarkets have agreed to put this film on their shelves because the people behind it haven't exactly been subtle." —Disney source via *The Daily Record*.

# MOUNT FEAR DIARY

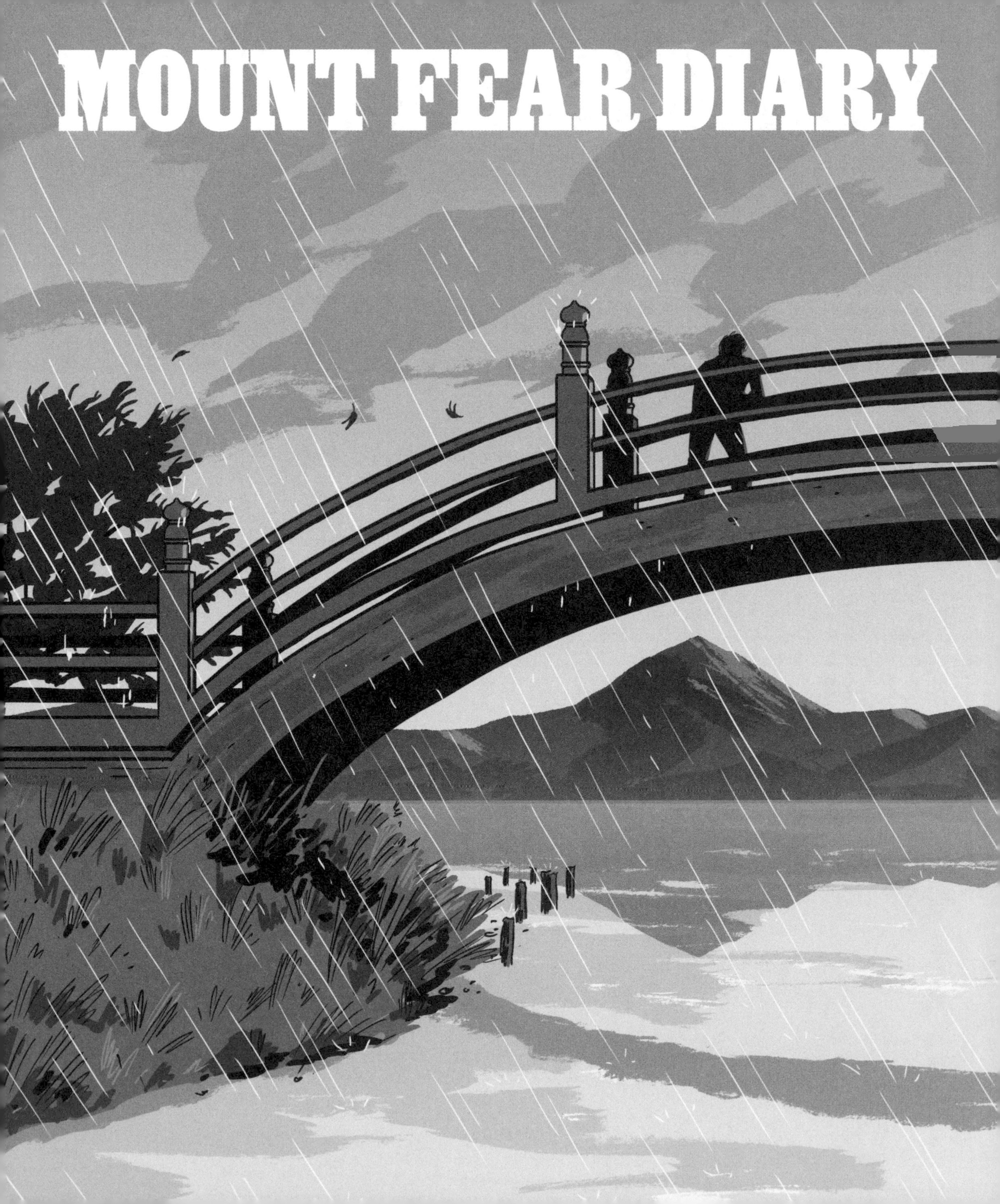

Reckoning with profound grief on the slopes of Osorezan—or "Mount Fear"—an active volcano that is believed to be a portal to the underworld.

by **JOSHUA HUNT**

illustrations by **JACK RICHARDSON**

n January 2023, while waiting to board a plane in Stockholm, I saw how swiftly grief can take hold of a person. In a quiet corner of Arlanda Airport, it unfolded before me like a scene from a movie: an older woman answered her cell phone, listened for a few moments to the voice on the other end, then burst into tears. Her anguish was so immediate, and so visceral, that it could only have been the worst kind of news—the end of a marriage, a dream, or a life. Not just any life, though: one so precious to her that its end was immediately comprehensible.

It was this immediacy that struck me as cinematic, because in real life, or at least in my life, death is many other things before it is something I can cry about. Last year, when my uncle Bill died of a heart attack at age fifty-seven, months passed before I could even conceive of his absence. He meant more to me than any other man, including my father, and yet his death was not at once fathomable to me. It landed with no impact I could make sense of; robbed of the clarifying weight of tragedy, I experienced his death first as an inconvenience. An obstacle. A disturbance that immediately complicated my life, or at least my career, which is what I had instead of a life. The instincts that had helped lift me out of poverty had also made it hard to slow down, and

so I lived as if on the run. Next stop: Tokyo, where I planned to cement my relationship with a big American magazine by writing the definitive profile of a major Japanese novelist.

These plans started taking shape in May 2022, when the lease on my apartment in Brooklyn, New York, was coming to an end. The rent was going up so much that renewing it seemed like a gamble I wasn't likely to collect on. Instead, I decided to do the responsible thing: put my stuff in storage, fly to Tokyo, and spend three months living in a modestly priced hotel while I wrote the story. I'd lived in Japan before, and going back after two years away seemed like the best shot I had at shaking off my malaise. It was also my best shot at producing a story that might take my writing career to the next level—a level that would put me in a position to take the occasional rent increase in stride.

By the end of the first week in June, I'd made it only as far as Manhattan, where a friend had invited me to house-sit while his family was on vacation. I was in their downtown apartment when I got the phone call about my uncle Bill. In bed but not yet asleep, I picked up the second of two late-night phone calls from my mom. Crying, and almost certainly a bit drunk, she told me that her little brother was gone, and all I could say was "Oh no." When our call ended, a little after midnight, I couldn't sleep, so I listened to old voicemail messages from my uncle. The most recent one

was dated December 25, 2021: "Merry Christmas, Josh. I love you. It's Uncle Bill. Hope you're having a wonderful day. Talk to you later. Bye."

I was meant to visit him three weeks after he left that message, but on the morning of my flight to Juneau, Alaska, I tested positive for COVID-19. I'd contracted the virus while working on a story in New Mexico—my first profile for the magazine I hoped to impress by flying halfway around the world to interview a novelist. While listening to old messages from my uncle, I dwelled bitterly on two unfulfilled promises I had made when calling to say I couldn't make it home in January: the first was that I would get to Alaska and see him again soon; the second was that he was going to love the profile I had been working on in New Mexico. It ended up being published ten days after he died.

With my flight to Japan booked, and my nonrefundable accommodations paid for in advance, I had a narrow window for making it to the potlatch that would serve as my uncle Bill's memorial. In Tlingit culture—our culture—the memorial potlatch has traditionally served as both a funerary ritual and a proto-capitalist one; for centuries, our departed were sent on their way with singing, dancing, food, and an ostentatious display of the wealth they would leave behind for others. These days, the banquets tend to resemble any other family cookout, and not many of our people have much wealth to leave behind. A few years ago, I met a man who put off his dad's potlatch long enough for the carving of a large memorial totem, which struck me as the height of Tlingit

*This story was supported in part by the Economic Hardship Reporting Project.*

opulence. My uncle Bill had left nothing behind, though, because he'd had so little, and because he had shared what little he had so freely. His potlatch proceeded as soon as a small wooden box with an image of an orca was carved to receive his ashes. By that time, though, my window of opportunity for attending had closed.

My mom sent me an announcement for the memorial service, which I perused on my phone during a layover on my way to Tokyo. In a quiet corner of Los Angeles International Airport, a dull pain grew sharper as I stared at the photograph they had chosen. It shows my uncle Bill standing

*Then, before he could explain himself any further, the aurora borealis began slithering across the night sky, and I could see with my own eyes how gods were born.*

on a beach on the outskirts of Juneau, bathed in sunlight passing through the sieve of an overcast sky. It is October 28, 2021, and in a few hours he will drive me to the airport for the last time. First we drive back to town, though, and along the way a double rainbow appears in the distance. He slows the pickup truck, then eases it over to the side of the road. He makes a dumb joke and asks me to take a picture of the two rainbows. When I send it to him later, I include another photo I took just a bit earlier. In it he is standing on the beach, dressed in jeans and a Carhartt shirt, smiling like he can already see the rainbows waiting just up the road.

I started speaking to my uncle almost as soon as he was gone. It began with the kind of question a child might ask: "What am I going to do without you?" In the days and weeks that followed, I kept talking, not incessantly, but often, and not loudly, but audibly, in the same way I might say "butter" or "milk" while reminding myself what to buy while shopping. The difference was that I was now speaking to some presence outside myself—not a being and not a void, nor a mere memory.

What started as a monologue came to feel like it was one side of a conversation that could never be made whole. I said whatever was on my mind, mostly, but some things came up over and over again. I repeated them while staring at the walls of my hotel room after midnight: "I'm sorry I didn't come see you one last time." While walking through Yoyogi Park, in central Tokyo, on a bright midsummer afternoon: "I'm going to miss you so much." While watching the sun rise over the Sumida River: "Can you believe how beautiful this world is?"

Speaking to the dead can, for a short while, seem to place us outside the laws of nature—outside the rules governing time and space. Memories of the departed inform our conversations with their ghost, and from those conversations, new memories are born. In this way, a person who no longer has a body or a consciousness can be made to cling stubbornly to the present tense. Several weeks after his death, I felt like my uncle was with me in Tokyo, seeing things he'd never had the chance to see when he was alive. His presence was so real to me that there were times when

I wanted to turn and speak over my shoulder, as if he were lagging behind, just out of view. This was comforting for a while. But as weeks turned into months, these conversations started to feel less like coping than a form of denial, so I decided some kind of exorcism was necessary. I bought a small black notebook at a stationery store, thinking I might better process my grief by keeping a diary. For weeks, I carried it with me at all times, but the words did not come.

Then, by pure chance, a friend told me about a place called Osorezan. We were talking about how my interviews with the Japanese novelist had finally been scheduled, which meant I was free to leave town until it was time to meet with her. Getting beyond Tokyo's city limits was something I hadn't done often enough when living in Japan, which I regretted, and since grief feeds on regret, it seemed like a trip to the countryside might do me good. I told my friend I wanted to head north and escape the summer heat, preferably somewhere out of the ordinary, and he mentioned Osorezan. Before I could ask about its extraordinary moniker—literally "Mount Fear"—he told me: "It's not a nickname."

It was his Japanese wife who had visited Osorezan, he told me, and she had never forgotten its otherworldly landscape, which was supposedly a portal to the underworld. Atop this active volcano is a caldera from which eight peaks rise up around a sulphurous lake; one of these is the peak of Osorezan itself, while others, like Mount Jizo, are considered distinct. After digging around online, I read more about the sacred pilgrimage site

in the book *Discourses of the Vanishing* by Marilyn Ivy:

> It is a terrain deathly enough to deserve its name, for the object of dread or terror (osore) at this place is death. In northeastern Japan, Mount Osore has long been the final destination of the spirits of the dead, the ultimate home where the dead continue to live a shadowy parallel "life." Yet more than just the home of the dead, the mountain is a place of practices for consoling, pacifying, and communicating with them, particularly during one delimited period of the summer.

Traveling there during this period, I realized, might amount to something like the potlatch I so regretted missing. Here was my chance for closure, or at least a more appropriate venue for the unwieldy spectacle of sadness—a place where the tears might finally come. I grew eager, even anxious. Speaking to my uncle's ghost was a comforting habit that raised discomforting questions—not only about memory and how we tend to it, but also about the impermanence of that heightened state of being we call grief. To kill a ghost, after all, we need only ignore it for a little while. Before his departed, I hoped to say all that needed to be said, and so I bought a train ticket to Mutsu, a village that sits at the base of Osorezan, and I gave my little black notebook the name 恐山日記, or "Mount Fear Diary." In it I would write my thoughts as I prepared for the trip, and would try to put down on paper some of what I'd been feeling since my uncle died. I opened it to the first blank page, and at last the words came.

**Tuesday, August 9, 2022**
**5:11 a.m.**
**Ryogoku View Hotel, Tokyo**

*His life ended in a trailer park home in the Mendenhall Valley in Juneau, Alaska. Years earlier, my grandma Rose, his mother, died in the same room, maybe even in the same bed. At the opposite end of the same trailer, my aunt Wendi, his sister, died in her own bedroom after mixing prescription pills with alcohol.*

I was twenty-seven when my grandma Rose died, and poor enough that no one gave me a hard time about missing her funeral. A year later, when my aunt Wendi died suddenly, at age forty-two, I was still living paycheck to paycheck, and still unable to make it back to Alaska on short notice. In both cases, poverty absolved me from admitting the truth, which is that I was grateful for any excuse to keep my distance. Since I moved away from home, those who stayed had been through horrors I couldn't imagine and didn't want to think about. I could do nothing for them, and little for myself, other than keep my distance from the carnage.

Whenever I did find the courage—and the money—to go home, it was my uncle Bill who saved me from despair. Being strong enough to face the carnage, and to live in its midst, he knew when it was a good day to visit my mom or my aunt or my cousin, and he knew when it was a bad day. He could tell when seeing someone hungover, strung out, or in jail would be better

than not seeing them at all. He could sense when I was drifting away, and he knew how to keep me tethered to the family without making me feel like I was on the hook and being reeled in by intergenerational trauma.

I learned a lot of what I know about life from my uncle Bill, who taught me how to fish, how to enjoy nature, and how to get by without a father. When I was a kid, he was a commercial fisherman, with enough pocket money to spoil his favorite nephew. He took me to the movies, to the arcade, and out for burgers at the one fast-food restaurant in Petersburg, Alaska. After weeks or months at sea, he would come back into my life like a whirlwind, and have me over to his apartment to play Nintendo or watch boxing matches on his big color television set. Once, he took me to Seattle, where we visited the Space Needle and looked out on what seemed like the whole world.

After my family moved to Oregon, just as I was starting middle school, I began to spend my summers with Uncle Bill in Alaska. He had moved to Juneau by then, and helped me get my first summer job there. When I got fired, he helped me get my second summer job, and with a minimum of preaching. His life had changed a great deal: after seeing his best friend go overboard and drown, he gave up commercial fishing for a less profitable job in construction. He had also given up the drinking that had failed to help him get over the tragedy. Going to church helped him stay sober in those days, and I often went with him, even though I found it boring.

My own relationship to Catholicism began and ended with a Saint

Christopher necklace my grandma Rose gave to me as a child. It was a curious possession—one that I prized as a gift and as a kind of talisman, even though I never came to believe in any church or any god. Jesus and the saints were as corny to me as the rituals of drumming, dancing, and singing I'd grown up with as a Tlingit. Once, and only once, I had felt I was in the presence of the divine: When I was seventeen or eighteen, and visiting Juneau for the winter, my uncle Bill took me to a quiet cove far outside the city, where we stood halfway between the tide and the tree line, taking in the view. It was three or four in the morning, the air was cold and clear, and the moon lit up the stretch of ocean between us and another island in Alaska's southeastern archipelago. It was a miraculous sight, but not the only thing my uncle had in mind when he rousted me from bed in the middle of the night.

"I thought we might be able to see the northern lights," he said. Then, before he could explain himself any further, the aurora borealis began slithering across the night sky, and I could see with my own eyes how gods were born.

**Wednesday, August 10, 2022**
**7:52 a.m.**
**Ryogoku View Hotel, Tokyo**

*For years, it was more than my career and living overseas that kept me away from Alaska. You never really escape poverty, but not calling home can be an escape from the ceaseless flood of bad news that makes it harder to move on with your own life. It took me years to realize it, but I'm now convinced that this partly accounts for how*

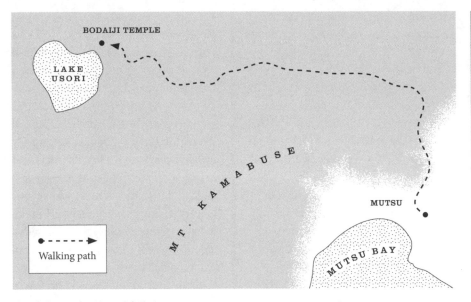

*The author's journey from Mutsu to Lake Usori.*

*at home I've always felt in Japan: an island country with a predominantly fish and seafood diet where religious and social rituals emphasize animistic gods; a place where people see the mountains and ocean and forest as living beings. Spiritual places filled with ghosts and monsters—the way my Tlingit ancestors saw the natural world.*

*Living in Japan, I could be foreign, anonymous, and far from family misfortune while enjoying the benefits of a place that felt both exotic and familiar. Furthermore, at matsuri (festivals) I was able to connect with aspects of Tlingit celebrations I'd always been too embarrassed or even ashamed to enjoy—like the Tlingit, Japanese people celebrate community through dance, drumming, chanting, and eating. Like us, they wear ritualistic clothes that hint at a simpler past for these celebrations. Through Shinto rituals and practices, I learned to see the beauty in Tlingit culture and traditions.*

*Having learned to appreciate my culture, I tried also to better appreciate my*

*family. There are still lots of tears, especially with my mom, but it felt good to be going home more often. It even felt good to cry together. With Uncle Bill, though, there weren't any tears—we spent our time together laughing, talking, exploring the outdoors, and recalling a lifetime of good memories. Good memories are the only kind I have with Uncle Bill.*

On a warm evening in August 2013, while working as an unpaid intern at the Tokyo bureau of *The New York Times*, I headed to a neighborhood bon matsuri on my way home. I'd been in Japan for about a year, studying at a university in Tokyo, and had come to feel very much at home there. The sense that this was in any way connected to my identity as an Alaska Native didn't occur to me until late summer, however, when the Buddhist Obon rituals emerge in traditions as varied as dancing at festivals and cleaning the headstones at the graves of one's ancestors. The

realization was fleeting: surrounded by hundreds of local people dressed in summer kimonos, singing, dancing, and eating food sold by vendors, I thought for a moment about some relatives who had passed on.

Two years later, after finishing up graduate school in New York City, I returned to Tokyo for a job as a foreign correspondent at Reuters. My love for the city deepened, as did my love for the neighborhood where I lived. One of Tokyo's paradoxical charms is that it is a city of vibrant communities built around train stations and markets and temples, each with a sense of intimacy and connectedness one would not expect to find in the world's largest metropolitan area. My favorite neighborhood landmark was the local Shinto shrine, called Shōin Jinja, after the nineteenth-century educator and activist Yoshida Shōin. In the Shinto religion—*Shinto* literally means "the way of the gods"—deities are all around us, animating the spirits of objects and places and creatures. After death, mortals like General Nogi Maresuke and Yoshida Shōin can be deified as well, making Shinto an ideal religion for warriors and intellectuals alike.

Throughout the summer and fall of 2015, I visited my local shrine a few times each month, but never gave much thought to what appeal it held for me. It was beautiful, like most shrines, and peaceful. But there was something else I had admired about Shinto since learning about it in a college Japanese literature course—something to do with its emphasis on actions rather than professions of faith, which had always struck me as in invitation to hypocrisy. This emphasis on rituals, gestures, and charms associated with shrines has to do with the shifting importance placed on Shinto and Buddhism over time; centuries ago, when state-sponsored Shinto was abandoned in Japan, thousands of shrines throughout the country were left to find new ways of supporting their activities. What saved them were festivals, where locals spent money on food and on religious charms and services. Adherence to the Shinto religion became entirely transactional, which appealed to me enormously as a lifelong skeptic with Christian relatives who had spent years asking me to profess faith in things I couldn't bring myself to believe. A general reverence for nature and a few coins in the prayer box was all that Shinto asked of me.

In Japan, my expectations of religious practice were inverted: in contrast to Americans, who profess belief in principles they don't adhere to, Japanese people often claim not to believe in the Shinto and Buddhist rituals they practice. My own first experiment with Shinto practices came on the second day of January in 2016, when I went to my local shrine and bought a hamaya. These ceremonial "evil-crushing arrows" are made from a narrow cylinder of wood with white fletching and white paper wrapped around the shaft. For about fifteen dollars, you can buy a pair of them to place in your home on a desk or a mantle, where they ostensibly absorb whatever bad luck might befall you throughout the year. When January comes again, and it's time for hatsumōde—the first shrine visit of the year—you buy a new hamaya and leave the old one in a pile at the shrine, where it will be ritually burned as a means of

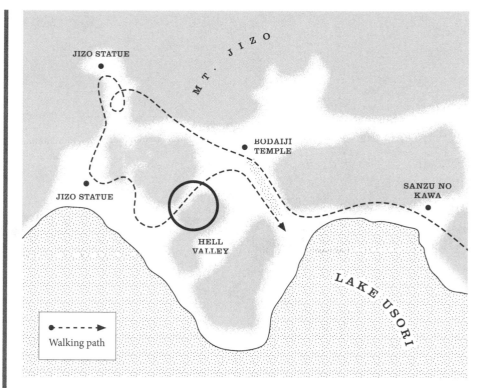

*The author's path along the shore of Lake Usori.*

destroying whatever ill fortune it has absorbed throughout the year.

What seemed like a novel way of participating in local life took on a different kind of significance the following January, when I was away from Japan for an extended work trip in the United States. Unable to bring the hamaya to my local shrine for burning, I kept them with me as I traveled. At first I regarded the fragile objects as precious but powerless, like the Saint Christopher necklace I was given as a child; they were something I could show my relatives as a means of illustrating the charm and exoticism of my new home overseas. But when the new year arrived, I found myself troubled by the unfulfilled ritual: buying the hamaya had somehow led me to buy into the mythology behind it. Like my

Japanese friends, I was unwilling to admit that I believed in its power, and yet, I was equally unwilling to treat the object as if it were powerless. And so, through a cynical cash transaction, I came closer than ever before to professing faith in an organized religion.

**Sunday, August 14, 2022**
**10:29 p.m.**
**Ryogoku View Hotel, Tokyo**

*O*n Friday morning I went to see a kabuki play at the Kabukiza Theater in central Tokyo. The second play of the morning/afternoon program was The Game of One Hundred Ghost Tales. *August is the traditional month for ghosts, spirits, and murder in kabuki performances. It is also the month of the Obon holiday, for which people throughout Japan return to their*

ancestral villages and hometowns to visit the graves of their ancestors—to tend and commune with them. It is a festive holiday with lots of dancing and lanterns. The Game of One Hundred Ghost Tales *also featured lots of dancing and lanterns. Its theme was the centuries-old tradition of lighting one hundred lanterns and gathering to tell ghost stories and supernatural tales. A lantern is extinguished after each tale, and it is believed that a real ghost will appear after the final lamp goes out; for that reason, one lantern is usually left burning when the evening concludes.*

*The play featured many tales of famous yurei (ghosts) and yokai*

*Within sight of the beach and the mountain range, I built a small pile of stones. While I did this, I thought of my uncle Bill—of the good and unique and brave and curious person he had been.*

*(spirits/monsters). One was the kappa—humanlike turtle creatures said to live in rivers, where they eat cucumbers and engage in sumo wrestling. They are said to menace humans and even remove a mythical organ called shirikodama by pulling it out through the human victim's anus. Kappa have a monk-like haircut, and the bald spot atop their heads supposedly holds water; being that they derive their power from water, they must keep this bowl-like indentation filled with water while away from the river. As such, it's said that you can defeat a kappa by bowing deeply to him—a gesture of courtesy he's obliged to return,*

*thereby spilling the water from atop his head and losing his supernatural powers.*

*Seeing the kappa do his dance, I thought of the kushtaka—a "land otter man" from Tlingit mythology. In ancient times, both spirits must have served a similar purpose: to keep children from falling into rivers and drowning. My grandparents very much believed in the kushtaka. In fact, my grandfather claimed to have encountered one while out trapping on an island near where I grew up. I made him tell me the story when I was young, after hearing it secondhand from my grandma. He did so reluctantly.*

When I was five or six, my grandma Rose told me about the time my grandpa Herb encountered the kushtaka. It happened while they were living in Petersburg, when she was pregnant with her first child. My grandfather had taken his skiff to an island across the channel, left it on the beach, and then walked through a valley that cut across the length of the island, where his otter traps were set. My grandmother usually went along with him, but she had decided to stay home that day because of her approaching due date. In previous weeks, her pregnancy had slowed her down on these trips. She found herself stopping to rest more often, each time calling out: "Herb! Wait up!"

When my grandpa first heard my grandma's voice, while walking through the valley, he thought nothing of it—until he remembered she was waiting for him at home. Each time he looked back in the direction her voice came from, he saw nothing, and sensed only an eerie silence in the surrounding forest. He began rushing through checking the traps, then decided to abandon his work altogether when her voice kept calling out to him: "Herb! Wait up!" He turned to walk back to his boat, but whenever he moved toward the shore, his head grew cloudy. It cleared only when he stopped and took a seat. He felt an overwhelming urge to lie down and sleep. The sense that he was not in control of his own mind ceased after he fired his rifle into the air, at which point the forest exploded with activity, as if every animal on the island were thrashing in the trees and bushes at the same time.

He ran back to the beach, returned home in his skiff, and never went back to the island to collect his otter traps.

**Friday, August 19, 2022**
**2:48 p.m.**
**Yoyogi Park, Tokyo**

*About an hour ago, while walking through the wooded areas of this magnificent park encircling Meiji Jingu shrine—a shrine for the Meiji Emperor—I felt very strongly that my uncle Bill was with me. So strong was this sensation that I stopped along a quiet brushed-gravel trail, which I had to myself in that moment, and I spoke: "Well, what do you think of this, Uncle Bill?"*

When I last visited my uncle Bill, he seemed in some way depleted. Even in middle age, when his hair had thinned and his trim, muscular physique had started to soften, he'd remained strong. Vigorous. It was clear something had happened since my previous visit, in February 2021, when he'd been healthy enough to hike through knee-high snow for hours as we crossed a frozen lake to reach the Mendenhall Glacier—a spontaneous effort he made in tennis shoes, after I'd casually mentioned wanting to put my hands on the glacier again one day. He did it without breaking a sweat. By the time I made it back to see him, in October 2021, he seemed sluggish and easily worn out. All he would say, though, was that he'd had his gallbladder removed and had to be more careful about what he ate.

But there were signs of something more going on. He'd become obsessed with documentaries about medical miracles and mysteries. On Facebook, he once made a cryptic post alluding to a cure sometimes being worse than the disease. Later, I would learn that he needed surgery for an enlarged heart. It scared him enough that he put it off, and he told just a few people, including my mother. He often refused to talk about it even with her. His behavior was something I could relate to, not having been to a doctor in several years. But it also made me wonder whether a single honest conversation might have saved his life.

Despite his declining health, he remained an outdoorsman, with a sense of the natural world that often seemed supernatural. One afternoon during my final visit, we stopped at a cove outside town, where he took one look at the water and guessed that crab would soon be there. In fact, early as it was for crab season, he said it was likely a few of them could already be found in one particular stretch of water. With my indulgence, he grabbed his fishing pole, and we walked onto a rocky point from which he could barely cast out to the meter-wide spot in question; since crabs are usually caught using baited traps, not fishing poles, I had no idea what he meant to do, until he cast once, twice, three times, before pulling in a crab he had somehow hooked. He smiled like a Little Leaguer after walloping a home run, then threw the crab back into the water. Later he said, "That was so cool," as if it were a card trick, when in fact it was one of the most amazing things I'd ever witnessed.

### Saturday, August 20, 2022
### 6:51 p.m.
### Ryogoku View Hotel, Tokyo

I *last saw my uncle Bill in October 2021. It was a ten-day visit. We were supposed to go halibut fishing, but his outboard for his skiff was in the shop for repairs. Still, we saw a lot of each other. We went out to eat often; my mom made beer-battered halibut for dinner at his house one night; and of course we drove out the road to enjoy the woods and beaches.*

*One night I took him out for dinner at one of Juneau's fancier restaurants—a place downtown called Salt. I loved being able to treat him to dinner, because he'd bought me so many meals throughout my life. And yet the fact that I now made more money than him did nothing to blunt his generosity. Because I'd only packed tennis shoes, and because it was raining quite a lot during my visit, Uncle Bill bought me a pair of XTRATUF rain boots—a necessary part of the Southeast Alaska "uniform." They kept my feet dry, but more than that, they made me feel like less of a tourist, like I was not so disconnected from my home and its culture even after two decades spent living*

elsewhere. *"You're Alaskan," my uncle Bill told me whenever I said I felt like a tourist. "You'll always be an Alaskan, Joshua."*

On a cloudy morning at the end of August, I carried my grief to a mountaintop near the northernmost tip of Japan's main island, at the center of the Shimokita Peninsula, where hell sits in a blackened caldera. Seeing it requires no act of imagination or leap of faith; Osorezan is a place as real as the pain that had brought me there. In antiquity, the Indigenous Ainu people called it Usoriyama, which to their early Japanese colonizers meant "cavernous mountain"—an apt description of the steaming, otherworldly abyss that formed near the peak of this active volcano when it erupted some twenty thousand years ago. Since the late eighteenth century, around the time of its last eruption, it has been called Osorezan, or "Mount Fear."

From the nearest train station, in the village of Mutsu, my walk to Osorezan took nearly four hours. The lonesome road was lined with tall trees that seemed to hold back the vast darkness of the forest. Beneath those trees, every few hundred feet, small statues of the Buddhist deity Jizō Bosatsu sat like lawn ornaments keeping watch at the edge of human existence. Behind them was a place beyond serenity, where the quiet of the forest was so intense that the sounds of rushing water and restless animals seemed faintly orchestral; in front of them was the road, where every so often faces stared back from the windows of a small city bus bound for the mountaintop Bodaiji temple, on the shores of the sulfurous and acidic Lake Usori. A tape recording told

passengers what they already knew—that "Osorezan is a place with many spirits."

The bus passed me twice as I made my way toward the caldera atop Osorezan, where Bodaiji and Lake Usori sit in the shadow of eight glorious peaks. Damp with sweat and rain, I wondered if the bus passengers could perceive the spirit walking with me. It had been there for eighty-five days, mute, but so real to me that I addressed it aloud. So real to me that the following week, while caught in a sudden downpour on the streets of Tokyo, I would burst into tears and thank it for the last gift it gave me: a sorrow deep enough to draw me back for the next funeral, and the next birthday, and all those other occasions when being together is more important than being free from pain.

### Tuesday, August 30, 2022
### 3:33 p.m.
### On Mount Fear

I*t started raining about 3 km from the bridge that symbolizes the border between our world and the underworld. Not a hard rain: a drizzle that almost made me feel as though I was back home in Southeast Alaska. Clouds filled the sky and mist clung to the surrounding mountain peaks. A short while before you reach the bridge, a powerful sulfurous smell rises up from a creek running toward the bubbling, poisonous lake. After that creek comes a modest river, over which the aforementioned bridge stretches—not a big bridge, but one with an impressive arch to it.*

*The river is called Sanzu no Kawa, which literally means "River of Three Crossings." In Japanese Buddhist*

# BOY WITH THORN

*by Jesse Nathan*

Wedged in my plantar fascia's rivers
of tissue, the tip of a spike from the locust
tree—some long as a boning knife—whose
thorn evolved to ward off long gone
mammoths, and who's
yet to realize
their absence.

---

mythology, it could be compared to the River Styx. Before reaching the afterlife, dead souls must cross the river at one of three points: Deep, snake-infested waters; a shallow ford suitable for wading; or the bridge. How one crosses into the underworld is determined by the weight of one's sins. The toll for crossing was six mon, according to Japanese Buddhist tradition, hence the practice of placing this fee in the casket of the deceased. Approaching the bridge, it's easy to see how Japanese came to believe the river beneath me, in rural Aomori Prefecture, was the real Sanzu no Kawa. Its waters are streaked with yellow and brown clay and it smells strongly of sulphur; the river, like Lake Usori, which it feeds, appears calm from a distance, but up close, you can see that the waters are punctuated by small fissures through which water heated by Mt. Osore, an active volcano, bubbles up to the surface. The result is eerie—like a thousand bubbling cauldrons set out upon the lake, shooting steam and poisonous gasses into the air.

Osorezan's peak is visible opposite the bridge over Sanzu no Kawa. It is a breathtaking sight—not fearsome at all, but gorgeous. Opposite the peak, just beneath Mt. Jizo, on the other side of Lake Usori, sits Bodaiji Buddhist temple. It's a short walk past the bridge. Walking to the temple—walking up Osorezan—took about three and a half hours. The road up the mountain is paved but lonely. It is also quite steep. The entire journey ultimately takes 13 hours.

Walking up Osorezan, the forest on each side of the road was dense and dark. Often one side was a valley, while the other rose up steeply like a castle wall covered in moss and dirt and trees. The trees in particular were unbelievably gorgeous. More than once I said out loud: "Have you ever seen anything so beautiful?" Being alone, I took many opportunities to dialog with my uncle Bill. I spoke to him for most of the way up, in fact, though he did not speak back. Mostly I rambled, but it always came back to the same basic thought, which I returned to again and again: "I miss you

so much." Every kilometer or so, stone Jizō statues sat covered in red or white scarves, sometimes with small offerings or piles of stones at their feet.

I was exhausted by the time I reached Bodaiji, where six grand statues of Jizō Bosatsu sit in a line at the edge of the parking lot. At the entrance, I paid 500 yen for a ticket and received a pamphlet along with it. It begins with a section titled "Legend and History," which suggests that myth is as important as fact within these temple walls:

> About 1200 years ago, the Japanese Buddhist priest Ennin was studying Buddhism in China. One night, he had a mysterious dream. In the dream a holy monk said to him: "When you return to Japan, go eastward. You will find a sacred mountain in 30 days' walk from Kyoto. Carve a statue of the Bodhisattva Jizō and propagate Buddhism there."

Ennin returned to Japan. In spite of various hardships, he traveled through many provinces on foot in the hope of finding the sacred mountain. Finally he came to the mountainous Shimokita Peninsula. There he found a place which met all the conditions required to be the sacred mountain for which he had been looking. It was this mountain, Osorezan.

Lake Usori sits at the center of the area known as Osorezan. Surrounding it are eight peaks rising up over the white sand and volcanic rock that line the shores of Lake Usori—eight peaks representing, for Buddhists, the eight petals of the lotus root symbolizing the Buddha. "In its central area," the pamphlet reads, "there are 108 ponds of boiling water and mud, which correspond to the 108 worldly desires and the hells linked to each of them."

Inside the outer walls of the temple, stone pathways lead to bathhouses and prayer halls. They are as impressive as any temple I've seen. But small touches hint at the Buddhist hellscape beyond the temple walls—statues of demons and a grotesque turtle that looks like some kind of monster. Beyond the main hall, which sits at the end of a long, straight path beginning at the main entrance, an unpaved path beckons. The landscape is stark: Massive volcanic rock formations erupt from the earth to create winding walkways leading up, down, left, right; in the shadow of the beautiful green mountain peaks, the landscape only looks more hellish.

After trekking over and across various volcanic formations, many still leaking steam through blackened fissures, I ventured back to the area closest to Mt. Jizō. There the landscape flattened out but remained coarse and strewn with volcanic rubble. Along with miniature Jizō statues, visitors had stacked piles of stones all across this rough and charred terrain. Some of them had the names of lost loved ones written on the stones; others had pinwheels or straw sandals placed alongside them as playthings for the souls of dead children. It is an incredibly eerie sight to behold, however kind the gesture. Beyond this area, near the slopes of Mt. Jizō, an enormous statue of the bodhisattva is perched on a stone carving of a lotus flower, which itself sits on an enormous stone base atop seven stone steps. It is a gorgeous and striking representation of the Buddha rescuing souls trapped between heaven and hell.

Standing before this great Jizō statue,

I said a prayer for the soul of my uncle Bill. Turning around, the path that led me there was on my left. On my right was an increasingly sandy path leading toward the shores of Lake Usori. I took it. Along the wide-open path, I was reminded of walking along the beaches of Southeast Alaska with my uncle Bill, exploring tide pools at the point where rocks give way to sand. This landscape looked somewhat like that, but instead of tide pools there were jagged wounds through which steam shot out of the earth and pools where hot poisonous water or mud gathered and boiled.

Several crows assailed one of the many small Jizō statues sitting in this part of the temple grounds. Walking past them, it was easy to see how people decided they were harbingers of something ominous. Beyond them, I found another Jizō statue sitting on a white-sand beach lining Lake Usori. Instead of praying to this Jizō, I found myself talking to my uncle once again, telling him how much I missed him. In the distance, a stunning mountain range stretched out across the landscape on the other side of the lake, with Osorezan itself in the center. It was now raining harder and the mist that hung over the top of the mountain range reminded me very much of Southeast Alaska. Of home.

I began crying—not sobbing, like I had been throughout the day, but really crying hard. Within sight of the beach and the mountain range, I built a small pile of stones. While I did this, I thought of my uncle Bill—of the good and unique and brave and curious person he had been. Kind. Strong. Capable. Honest. Loving. Turning back toward the mountain range, with the pile of stones behind me, I began talking to them. Crying, I said: "I

don't know what I'm going to do without you, Uncle Bill. But if I have to say good-bye to you, I want to do it right here." My heart swelled to the point of bursting at the beauty of this place. I went on: "This world is so beautiful and I can't believe that you're not a part of it anymore."

For the next fifteen minutes, I stood there crying on the beach, where my tears mingled with the falling rain. Before long, I would have to walk back to the parking area, where a public bus would take me down the mountain. I was too exhausted to walk, and if I missed the bus it would add several hours to my return trip. I wasn't ready to say goodbye, but I was even less ready to spend several more hours in this haunted place. I stared at the landscape for as long as I could without blinking; I took in the unfathomable beauty of the scenery where my uncle Bill's pile of stones sat. I wished he could see it all through my eyes, then realized I was seeing it through his.

The path leading back to the main entrance was all burnt rocks and volcanic formations: the very picture of hell. I tried not to look over my shoulder at the mountain range beyond the lake, hoping to preserve the memory of how it looked from the pile of stones I'd made for my uncle Bill. But I couldn't help myself: Again and again, I turned back for one last look at that magnificent sight. Eventually, I crested a hill made from twisted and burnt volcanic rock. Coming down the other side of it, I turned around for one more look at the last view I would ever share with my uncle Bill—but by then it was obscured by the hill I'd just crossed over, and instead of paradise, all I could see was hell. I kept on walking, though, and soon that, too, was behind me. ✶

# A VIRTUOSIC NEW POETRY COLLECTION FROM SALLY WEN MAO, "A CONSISTENTLY INSPIRING AND EXCITING VOICE" (MORGAN PARKER)

In *The Kingdom of Surfaces*, award-winning poet Sally Wen Mao examines art and history—especially the provenance of objects such as porcelain, silk, and pearls—to frame an important conversation on beauty, empire, commodification, and violence. In lyric poems and wide-ranging sequences, Mao interrogates gendered expressions such as the contemporary "leftover women," which denotes unmarried women, and the historical "castle-toppler," a term used to describe a concubine whose beauty ruins an emperor and his empire. These poems also explore the permeability of object and subject through the history of Chinese women in America, labor practices around the silk loom, and the ongoing violence against Asian people during the COVID-19 pandemic.

At its heart, *The Kingdom of Surfaces* imagines the poet wandering into a Western fantasy, which covets, imitates, and appropriates Chinese aesthetics via Chinamania and the nineteenth-century Aesthetic Movement, while perpetuating state violence upon actual lives. The title poem is a speculative recasting of *Through the Looking-Glass*, set in a surreal topsy-turvy version of the eponymous China-themed 2015 Metropolitan Museum of Art Gala. *The Kingdom of Surfaces* is a brilliantly conceived call for those who recognize the horrors of American exceptionalism to topple the empire that values capital over lives and power over liberation.

## AVAILABLE AUGUST 1ST

GRAYWOLF
PRESS

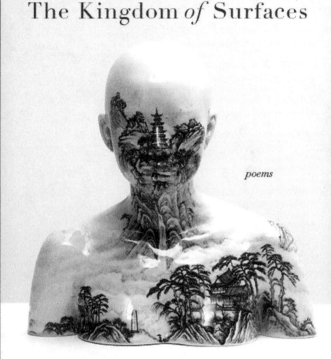

The Kingdom *of* Surfaces

*poems*

Sally Wen Mao

# PLACE

## BOTSWANA SAFARI

*by Lucy Corin*

FEATURES:

✶ Frogs that sound like xylophones
✶ Competent warthogs
✶ Luxuriating giraffes

I spent a few days watching wild animals I know practically nothing about.

Hippos—two, three, or a dozen, depending on the size of the waterhole they stand dozing in all day—do this:

"Move over."
"You move over."
"OK."
[Time, time, time.]
"No, really, you move over."
"OK, but I don't like it."
"OK."
[Time, time.]
"Actually, you move over."
"Uh-uh."
[Time.]
"OK."

Warthogs and wildebeests appear on film to be blocky, stiff creatures, and their blocky stiffness makes them seem stupid and humorless. But they're not. They are graceful, competent, and tell jokes.

When two young impalas are sparring, just testing each other out, measuring, they do it in total sync. Butt, butt, butt, then stop, look around, then butt, butt, stop, look around. They are so in tune with each other, and the timing of an antelope's need to look for danger is so precisely understood, that the levels of being are stark. They have to do this sparring. They just have to get it done. They have to understand the difference between each other. But no impala (I feel sure, based on practically nothing) is going to stab another impala while he is scanning for danger, because above all, they are impalas together, and so they look out.

Before the trip, I watched a video of a brutal fight between giraffes. Giraffes use their heads to beat each other. Partway through listening to David Attenborough's take on this, I tried to watch the video without listening to him. There's been so much stupid anthropomorphizing (*Look: they're married!*), and so much stupid—what should I call it?—dehumanizing?—of animals (*That murderer is an animal! He treats her like an animal!*), that I keep trying to look at animals as an act of cognitive decluttering. When dogs fight and cats fight it's—obviously—*very emotional*. I grew up around horses, and I've never seen a horse do *anything* without a legible emotion. But these giraffes—I could pause the video and walk right up to their faces and see nothing. I tried to perceive anger or fear in their bodies. If I ignored the blank-to-me looks on their faces, could I see emotion there? Focusing on just the bodies made them more coherent to me. The best thing about having bought TSA PreCheck is that I don't have to walk into that glass tube at the airport and lift my arms, because I can't lift my arms like that without feeling *Don't shoot* all through my body. Do giraffe faces simply not do what human faces do, muscularly? Or are they not feeling what I can understand as feeling? When one of them finally fell and the great neck followed, and then his poor head finally hit the ground, his eyes closed for a moment, and then, in the space of the closing of the eye, I thought I could see the feeling.

When I saw giraffes in the wild, I found it impossible to see them as other than voluptuously luxuriating—those necks and heavy-lidded eyes, of course, but mostly the vast haunches. The *flanks*. I enjoyed seeing them this way. It was like seeing an entire fantastical species of gorgeous, decadent ladies from another planet, and who doesn't want to see that? I didn't quite want to leave the human cultural history they were evoking for me. I feel like I can do that for a while without harming them, as long as I am prepared to let go.

The hyena, in people's effort to describe it, is part cat and part dog. I do not think it's right for Disney to have rendered an entire species as Nazis, so I was especially glad to be able

*Illustration by Madison Ketcham*

to see them. It is true that hyenas will eat a hyena that dies, and it's true that they sometimes walk around all day with their heads covered in blood. But *what's my problem with that?* I kept asking myself when I felt the repulsion. I didn't see them do either of these things, though I heard that other people on the trip had watched this happening. What I saw them doing was napping, walking around in the grass, looking powerful, and slipping, in their strangeness, away from my efforts to fix them with my mind.

I saw a lot of other animals and tried to keep track of them on a card with checkboxes. I saw: Baboon (chacma), Buffalo (African), Bushbuck, Cheetah, Eland, Elephant (African), Fox (bat-eared), Giraffe, Hare (scrub), Hippopotamus, Hyena (spotted), Impala, Jackal (black-backed), Jackal (side-striped), Kudu (greater), Lechwe (red), Leopard, Lion, Mongoose (banded), Monkey (vervet), Porcupine (great), Reedbuck, Springhare, Squirrel (African ground), Steenbok, Tsessebes, Warthog, Waterbuck, Wild Dog, Wildebeest (blue), Zebra (plains), but I could not even fathom the birds or the reptiles. And then there was a section for insects and plants. I felt an exhaustion in naming. I felt I was losing the animals as I tried to contain them in that way.

Today I read Zadie Smith ("Fascinated to Presume: In Defense of Fiction") and started Jane Bennett (*Influx and Eflux: Writing Up with Walt Whitman*). Both Smith and Bennett quote Whitman's line about multitudes, but Bennett quotes it without the parentheses, and Smith quotes it with the parentheses: "(I am large, I contain multitudes)." I had no idea that line has parentheses! Obviously, I did not really go for the Romantics. I'm kind of shocked that it isn't always emphatically disseminated within its parentheses, infinite regress and simultaneous expansion. I get that parentheses are a mouthful. I picture people passing the line along holding their hands in two crescent moons at their shoulders, trying to signify. I tried to remember if maybe the line occurs in the poem more than once. Maybe at first it was in its parentheses, but at some point got out. I don't have a copy of the poem in the house. I don't want to get into the internet. I asked a poet friend about all this. She cleared some of it up for me, but she also said there are multiple editions, lots of feelings around them.

I would watch the animals—an individual here, a group there—watching the way my mind wanted to read personality onto the effect of, say, a species with a big beak versus a species with a little beak, a broad brown stripe down a nose

rather than a narrow one. Watching myself being phrenological with them.

That may be why, after a day of looking, moving safely among many layers of my invasion of animal and human spaces within the violence of safari, then and now and beyond, I liked to stand on the little bridge to the camp as dusk accumulated, listening to the sound of xylophones. I knew the sound was frogs—(reed frogs, I learned)—because I grew up with tiny tree frogs that would sing so loudly that guests sometimes shut their windows tight, even in the summer, with no air conditioning, in order to sleep. What were the animals without me? I could stand on the bridge letting the idea of *animal* that people made vibrate in the reality of their sound. ✷

---

## SONGS GUILLERMO DIAZ ASKS PARKER POSEY TO RETRIEVE FROM HIS RECORD COLLECTION FOR HIS DEEJAY SET IN *PARTY GIRL* (1995)

✷ "You Make Me Feel (Mighty Real)," Sylvester
✷ "The Lover Who Rocks You (All Night)," India
✷ "Double Cross," First Choice
✷ "You Sexy Thing," Hot Chocolate
✷ "Hot Music," Pal Joey
✷ "X," Junior Vasquez
✷ "Up Down Suite," Madonna
✷ "My Jimmy Weighs a Ton," Jungle Brothers
✷ "Eric B. Is President," Eric B. & Rakim
✷ "The Nervous Track," Nuyorican Soul
✷ "Sex Drive," Grace Jones
✷ "Is It All Over My Face?" Loose Joints
✷ "Saturday Night," Whigfield
✷ "Sweet Pussy Pauline," Candy J
✷ "Activator (You Need Some)," Whatever, Girl
✷ "Flash Light," Parliament
✷ "Genius of Love," Tom Tom Club
✷ "You Used to Hold Me," Ralphi Rosario
✷ "Flip the Script," Gang Starr
✷ "Insomnia," Faithless

*—list compiled by Reid Van Mouwerik*

Putting one foot in front of the other until you arrive at a destination you may not have thought possible.

We're doing it our way, *little by little.*

little X little

littlexlittlewines.com

# GAIL SCOTT

[WRITER]

"I'M IN THE BATH AND I'M HAVING A GREAT TIME—
IS THIS POLITICAL?"

Canadian literary magazines mentioned in this interview:
*Tessera*
*La nouvelle barre du jour*
*CV2*
*Room of One's Own*

**G**ail Scott's most recent collection, Permanent Revolution: Essays *(Book\*hug Press), reads backward. It begins in the present, with Scott's experiments in language taking her to Paris, San Francisco, and, most recently, Obama-era New York. Part two returns to Montreal, where Scott got her start in the '70s as a writer, journalist, translator, and editor; in these older essays, Scott evokes the polyglot community she built with Nicole Brossard, Louky Bersianik, and France Théoret, sharing bottles of wine, arguing about Maurice Blanchot until midnight, and reading issues of* Tel quel *in the back of a Volkswagen van.*

*With variations on every way a sentence could be,* Permanent Revolution *has few constants, though it always makes room for friendship, politics, and language. It could be feminist, it could be queer, but it evades a fixed identity. It's liquid and subtle. As probing as Gertrude Stein, as lusty as François Rabelais, as analytical as Luce Irigaray, Scott seems forever in motion. Places and ideas fly by, leaving Scott's*

*Illustration by Kristian Hammerstad*

*readers wondering, like the curious revelers in Édouard Manet's* Masked Ball at the Opera: *Who is she?*

*I first read Scott in Paris in 2010. It was late summer, the apartment on the rue Jacob was shaded, dark. I had her fifth book—*My Paris, *written in present participles—a hypnotically shattered memoir of six months in the city, where Scott is wandering, loving women, and reading Walter Benjamin on a canapé. It wasn't until 2017 that I heard Scott read. She'd been invited to the University of California at Berkeley by the poets Daniel Benjamin and Eric Sneathen for a conference on New Narrative, a group of queer friends in San Francisco who wrote strange novels full of philosophy and desire. Wheeler Hall was cool in the heat of California's October, and poets crowded in to hear her, the windows opened to camphorous eucalyptus and the sweet nocturnal rush of Strawberry Canyon. Scott's voice was polished, smoky, English, French, Canadian, unplaceable. She read from her forthcoming book on New York,* Furniture Music *(Wave Books, October 2023), a lush conjuring of poetry, community, and protest in Lower Manhattan in the 2010s.*

*In August of 2019, I finally made it to Montreal—Scott's home of many years—but not before spending all of June and July fervently reading* Heroine, *her first novel. Has there ever been such a first novel? Its protagonist arrives in a new city in the "bottomless" '80s, speaks the wrong language, and makes a whole new way of being. It's a lucid romance of militant politics, borderless Eros, resistance in language, and flaneur aesthetics. Thirty years later, when strangers on the street in Montreal stopped my then boyfriend to tell him—in French, and very politely—how beautiful he was in his six feet, two inches of Gaultier Femme, we knew it was still Scott's city.*

*After a briefly bilingual correspondence, Scott and I mostly used English, which she said I spoke so correctly it sounded like my second language. (It isn't.) Between New York and Les Cantons de l'Est, near Montreal, we talked over Zoom about whether pleasure is political, why she's never wanted to be a feminist icon, and what it means to write from pure desire.*

—Dylan Byron

### I. AN ABSORBENT LANGUAGE

THE BELIEVER: We're speaking English. But we could have been speaking French. You grew up in a bilingual community near the Quebec border, and your most recent book, *Permanent Revolution*, describes this liminal space, lamenting: "In my town, Montréal, QC, it can feel like the French language is the survivor of 2 colonial impulses, Euro-French + continental English." Do you think English deserves a future in North America?

GAIL SCOTT: I laughed when I saw this question, thinking of francophone cohorts in Quebec, who would surely be tempted to shout a resounding "*Non!*" English has brutally sucked the energy out of peripheral groups—Indigenous people, for example, where the effort to impose English was actually homicidal. James Baldwin, who spoke the most elegant English imaginable, said he was speaking an enemy language. For me, writing mostly in English in the French part of North America, the chastening contradiction is that English is a great language to write in because it's so elastic and so absorbent of other cadences, other argots.

BLVR: You worked for the *Montreal Gazette* during the October Crisis of 1970, when the minister of labor and the British trade commissioner were taken hostage by the Front de libération du Québec. Your first novel, *Heroine*, set ten years later, includes many "felquiste" sympathizers, organizing in solidarity with Quebec's traditionally French-speaking, anti-English working class.

GS: Sympathizers not with terrorist methods, but with the felquiste manifesto of liberation for Quebec's francophone working class. English tried very hard to dominate French in Quebec, and almost succeeded in rubbing it out until that whole Quiet Revolution and post–Quiet Revolution period I write about in *Heroine*. One of the issues with writing on the cusp of another language is the ethics of doing this permeable thing that English does so well. When I wrote *Heroine*, I decided I was going to write a book that wouldn't make me ashamed with my francophone friends or my anglophone friends. I wanted to be socially consistent and in context, as opposed to doing a performance that basically ripped off or exoticized another culture.

BLVR: I guess the queer aspect is that speaking in other languages allows for code-switching, masks, masquerades.

GS: I know that when I'm talking to my francophone friends, I'm not the same person as when I'm speaking to anglophones.

In writing, this has meant trying to find the form or scaffolding that allows for an open reading of my work. This interest I have in languages predates feminist and queer factors. Yet it very much overlaps with queer performance—the notion of speech as performance is very present when you're switching languages.

BLVR: There's a certain rhythm to your speech—in English, in French—and your engagement with language strikes me as profoundly sonic. It's like you're listening while you're writing.

GS: Montreal has a different sound than any other city in Canada. I walk around Montreal all the time listening to people talk. When I was teaching at the University of Montreal, I loved to listen to the students, because they had the greatest slang—a way of slipping and sliding over language that was witty, self-aware, savvy, and porous, but not in the least deferential.

## II. "WRITING AS PURE DESIRE"

BLVR: Your work also draws on forms of dandyism and flânerie from francophone culture. At one point in *Permanent Revolution*, your English-speaking niece is incredulous that you're related to her, leading you to feel—in your "pointed boots," "black-+-white-striped sweater," and "at the moment trendy pants, cut wide at the hips + narrow at the ankles"—like a "misplaced dandy." Your work is political, but dandyism is about pleasure. Can pleasure also be political?

GS: I came along in the '70s, when my milieu in Montreal perceived the hedonism of '60s counterculture as lacking in political definition. One of our questions then, which I still find crucial, was: How can you democratize access to pleasure? Certainly problematic if you are doing three jobs a day to make ends meet.

BLVR: Pleasure seems to be everywhere in *My Paris*. Let me quote you: "Waking... A couple of tartines. No thought of lunch. Ditto way of moving. Trimmer. Red mop smooth. Strolling to Palais-Royal. Former home of Colette. Old hedonist. Knowing how to take pleasures of the body." Your evocation of Colette here seems not incidental.

GS: Yes, at the same time as we were trying to politicize everything, we began speaking of writing as pure desire. It was a Barthesian idea that seemed to pull in two directions at once. The thing that troubles me is that the pursuit of pleasure too often gets grounded in single-issue identity politics.

BLVR: Did you ever face resistance from your political communities because of the jouissance that drives your writing?

GS: *Jouissance* is a good word, it's totally jouissance, in the sense of losing the self in the pleasure of the process. When *Heroine* came out, another writer said to me, "This isn't a feminist novel. The women don't get along!" That was a raw comment. I haven't made it my goal to do the radical feminist anything; it's not who I am. Without multiple intersectional solidarities, there's practically always a backlash. There was a hell of a backlash against feminism in the '90s, and I'm worried it's going to happen to the Indigenous movement. As I say in *Permanent Revolution*: "rage accumulates."

BLVR: I remember you quoting a critic whose bewildered response to *My Paris* was that it must be some kind of "lesbian aesthetic." Without wanting to assign you an individual subject position as a "queer writer," I wonder whether being in queer community allowed you to engage with the pleasure-politics dialectic outside the puritanical, heterosexual left.

GS: The pleasure-killer was less puritanism than good old male-dominant heteronormality. Feminism started me down the slippery slope of demanding what I had always already wanted: freedom to dispose of my body, my drives, as I saw fit. Twenty seconds later I was in the lesbian camp. Also, Quebec is a francophone society, and there is a certain attention to pleasure—to dress, to food, to beautiful writing, to beauty itself—that's articulated very differently than in Ontario, for example. French literature was so instructive in that regard, be it Colette, [Roland] Barthes, [Marguerite] Duras, even that old Protestant [André] Gide, especially when he writes of queer desire. But is this pleasure political? It's hard to say, because isn't pleasure about being in the moment? I'm in the bath and I'm having a great time—is this political?

BLVR: I was reading *Permanent Revolution* on Riis Beach [in New York City], and when I saw that title ["The Smell of Fish"], I turned to my boyfriend and said, "Woah!" It's an adventurous book—a polyphony of essayistic forms. Do you know the poet Anne-Marie Albiach?

GS: Oh yes!

BLVR: She describes the breath of the poem, the body of the poem. Your prose always takes different shapes, almost like the varied approach of a lover.

GS: The essays in the second section of the book came from my women's writing group with Nicole Brossard and company. We wanted to project, in language, and without embarrassment, our own physical impulses. We knew this was a matter of form, that genre limits had to be crossed, that theory was part of the picture—[Monique] Wittig, [Julia] Kristeva, Irigaray. But also Barthes and [Jacques] Derrida. For me, a watershed book was Christine Buci-Glucksmann's book about the Baroque in reference to Walter Benjamin. At the same time, just before I wrote *Heroine*, I was reading [Sigmund] Freud. I was very interested in the relation between body and language, and very conscious that he wasn't doing it right as far as women were concerned. Speech for me is very close to the body, and speech is infinitive in the sense that it's always rearranging, retorquing, uncovering what is not quite conscious.

### III. LA SUJETTE

BLVR: Do you accept the idea of "women's writing"? You've alluded to some of the dissonances you feel with contemporary identity politics, the complexity of your subject position, your resistance to and your escape from—

GS: Protestantism.

BLVR: I was going to say *the category of women's writing*, but that too! You write in *Permanent Revolution*, "I don't think we have talked enough about the feminist/queer cusp." Earlier theorists like Wittig—whom you quote as saying, "Lesbians are not women"—really paid attention to specific social constructions of identity. Now it sometimes seems like everyone has to have a possibly intersectional but definitely

fixed subject position, and the work of art is expected to represent the subject position rather than question it.

GS: That's exactly my problem.

BLVR: How do you negotiate this more rigid moment in identity politics?

GS: You notice I cite Eileen Myles in the epigraph. I love their "I'm the gender of Eileen"—what freedom that gives everybody on the spectrum! Because we're all a little different in some respect, you know? At some point in *Permanent Revolution*, I call myself a "FE-male." What I'm saying is, I'm a woman, but I'm also a lesbian. I'm not necessarily a whole girl, even though I look like one. I have these different drives going on. I don't see how you can defend this identity versus that one. We're all moving and we're all evolving as we understand more about these things.

BLVR: How do you see your books tracking that movement over time?

GS: For me it comes down to various attempts at breaking the back of the commodity novel, with its heteronormative, nineteenth-century emphasis on the individual psychology

---

### VELÁZQUEZ PAINTINGS FEATURING A SMALL DOG

✭ *Dog and Cat*, 1650–60
✭ *Joseph's Bloody Coat Brought to Jacob*, 1630
✭ *Philip IV Hunting Wild Boar (La tela real)*, 1632–37
✭ *Portrait of Cardinal Infante Ferdinand of Austria with Gun and Dog*, 1632
✭ *Prince Baltasar Carlos in Hunting Dress*, 1635–36
✭ *Infante Felipe Próspero*, 1659
✭ *Las meninas*, 1656
✭ *Philip IV of Spain*, 1632–33
✭ *Prince Balthasar Carlos Dressed as a Hunter*, 1635–36
✭ *A Buffoon* [mistitled *Antonio the Englishman*], 1640
—*list compiled by Katherine Williams*

of characters around the family. It has to be broken down. It has to let in air. All my novels are an experiment with that. In *Heroine*, you have the spiral allowing the reader to be looking at the story from different angles all the time. Then in *Main Brides*, you've got the woman in a bar, and as she's becoming inebriated, she's imagining the stories of other women, but you don't really know if it's other women or if it's her, so there's fluidity between the figures. In *My Paris*, I tried to reduce the "I" to the smallest unit possible. To do that I used the present participle, because if you omit the active part of the verb, there's no big "I" left anymore—it really makes the text porous. And then in *The Obituary*, I tear it all apart, so you've got Rosine as the lesbian in the basement, as the fly on the wall, and also as the body on a bed.

BLVR: Presumably the complexity of your position also evolved from the Montreal feminist theory group you belonged to with Brossard, Louky Bersianik, France Théoret, Louise Cotnoir, and Louise Dupré. In your essay "The Virgin Denotes," you recall: "We wanted to circumvent *logos*. Without somehow abandoning a towering lucidity." How did you evade the masculine borders of theory?

GS: I feel like I got my theoretical education outside the university—in the left, and in the feminist movement. One advantage we had in Montreal was that we could read this stuff before it got translated. We were just gobbling it up all the time. The air was thick with theory and politics. And as feminists we were having no truck with masculine shortsightedness. We could decide to read only women philosophers for a time. But we were also well-informed. I remember I went on a camping trip one summer in a Volkswagen van. I spent the whole time reading back issues of *Tel quel*. It was a problem for me to leave the van. As for our writing group, once a month for about eight years we would get together. We would have a subject of conversation, half-playful but also serious. One of the ones I remember was "la sujette."

BLVR: The female subject?

GS: Playing on the idea of the female subject as the writing subject. But then we would each

write a semi-theoretical text—in French. We would have croissants, coffee, and discuss the texts. We would bring in all the stuff we were reading, and argue about what Kristeva meant here, or what Duras or Barthes or Blanchot meant there. Once we'd finished talking about the texts, out came the bottles of wine. I remember one meeting that went from twelve noon until twelve at night. You can't get a better education than that. It was such a great period. We were also trying to relate our reading and writing to feminist and social practice, because a lot of us were militants too. Louky [Bersianik] was the one who came up with the expression *écriture-au-feminin* [writing-in-the-feminine]. We didn't really like [Hélène] Cixous's *écriture feminine* [feminine writing]. Some of us were lesbians! And we were like, Are we "feminine"? It's like thinking there's something already there that you can describe. What is the feminine? We don't know. We don't know what the masculine is either. And Louky said, "I prefer the term *écriture-au-feminin*, because then you have the masculine as well as the feminine."

BLVR: Because the noun for "the feminine" is masculine in French?

GS: Try explaining that to an anglophone audience! But it's true. Putting it that way left some air and left some flexibility in the term. I think after a while both Nicole [Brossard] and I used the term less, but at least it was a stage. The feminine certainly still interests me from the point of view of desire and from the point of view of language.

BLVR: Several of the group's essays are collected in *Theory, A Sunday*. In the introduction, Lisa Robertson elegizes the Montreal scene as "mythic and galvanizing." What were its other reverberations?

GS: With women from English Canada, I cofounded a magazine called *Tessera*. We decided to piggyback on other literary magazines around the country, some French like *La nouvelle barre du jour*, as well as *CV2*, out of Winnipeg, and *Room of One's Own* in Vancouver, which allowed the discussions that were happening in French to seep out in translation.

BLVR: Were there intersections with gay writing communities? If I'm not mistaken, Yves Navarre lived in Montreal for part of the '80s.

GS: For some reason, that era in Quebec and the one just preceding produced a lot of queer writers. Marie-Claire Blais, for example. My immediate milieu in the larger poetry community had a lot of gay writers with whom we constantly collaborated. André Roy, who is today one of Quebec's most important poets. Jean-Paul Daoust. Michael Delisle, whom I translated. They were definitely part of the scene. They weren't in our group, but they were around *La nouvelle barre du jour*.

### IV. AN UNSTABLE AVANT-GARDE

BLVR: I was surprised to read in *Permanent Revolution* that you carried [Samuel] Beckett in your old, battered steamer trunk full of manuscripts and notes.

GS: The thing about Beckett was that I wanted to be taken seriously for my writing, because the work seemed to get reduced to a label: *Feminist. Lesbian. Leftie.* Whatever. It's not that I wanted to win the Nobel Prize—that would never even have crossed my mind. But I wanted to be an experimental prose writer whose work was taken seriously. I don't think those labels are as reductive and problematic now as they were when I was a young writer, but then it was really a way of saying, *Well, she's good enough for what she is*, you know?

BLVR: You write that your readings of Duras, Kristeva, Stein, Wittig, Brossard, Cixous, Emma Santos, and Sophie Podolski "confirm what we already feel—that to express the shape of our desire, our prose must lean toward poetry." I wonder how you negotiated the genre policing that seemed to have accompanied the gender (genre) policing.

GS: Poetry still teaches me how to write prose. I suppose my dream has always been to accomplish something of what poetry accomplishes, but also of what the novel accomplishes, because for me the novel also allows a social insertion, a working out. All of my novels are written in a social context that bears discussing. Every period requires a different kind of experimentation. Another writer whose work I love—and

this won't surprise you—is Viktor Shklovsky, especially *Zoo, or Letters Not about Love*. There is always the roar and insecurity of political rupture. As for policing the gender/genre thing, it's an ongoing battle in terms of institutional acceptance. There is prose and there is poetry, and never the twain shall meet.

BLVR: You talk about *Zoo* in *Permanent Revolution*.

GS: That line of Shklovsky's, "If a line continues without breeding with the non-esthetic, nothing is created," represents for me what a novel can do that poetry, probably, has more difficulty with. That's one reason I'm still a novelist. Anyway, I couldn't write a poem to save my life.

BLVR: I don't believe you.

GS: Or what I would consider a poem, anyway.

BLVR: Another context for *Permanent Revolution* is your encounter with San Francisco Bay Area writers Robert Glück and Carla Harryman. Here, too, the problem of story returns, with Language poets trying to dismantle first-person expression, and New Narrative writers queering it, putting in theory and body. How did the New Narrative group change your relationship to language?

GS: I got to know the San Francisco people in the '90s. One of my big problems in Quebec was that most of my friends had this principle that you shouldn't get too involved with English. So I hardly ever got really good feedback from my francophone cohorts about my English writing, and I was starving after a while. Meeting Carla [Harryman] was a big moment. She's a poet but she writes a lot of prose and I love her performance work. I see a kinship with Beckett. Then meeting New Narrative people like Bob [Glück], Camille [Roy], Kevin [Killian], and Dodie [Bellamy]—and, on the East Coast, Eileen [Myles]. It was just so thrilling for me. I knew that my work wasn't ever going to look like theirs exactly; it was coming from a different place. But I knew that we had things in common, not the least of which was the relationship of our queerness to our writing.

BLVR: I'm interested that you didn't mention Bruce [Boone].

GS: You know, I only met Bruce once. But having said that, I don't think his contribution is nearly as well known as it should be.

BLVR: I ask about Bruce particularly because he has such a complex engagement with French literature. You know he translated [Georges] Bataille and Pascal Quignard.

GS: I certainly recognize a kindred spirit in him. I have the impression that the juncture between art and politics happens around the same place in our writing.

BLVR: Excluding New Narrative, it seems like a lot of North American avant-garde poetics in the '80s, '90s, and maybe 2000s weren't grounded in real political community and became somewhat arid or academic. Are avant-garde writing procedures always politically liberatory?

GS: I think we have to stop expecting the notion of avant-garde to be a stable notion. Looking back at some people who have performed avant-garde functions, [Ezra] Pound opened doors in poetry and then became a fascist. Avant-garde for me always has to be viewed in context. There can be great stuff coming out of a certain moment, like Dada, or the surrealists. We owe so much to André Breton, but feminists don't like him, and he was homophobic up the you-know-what. He made René Crevel totally miserable.

BLVR: You've translated a number of friends, fellow travelers—Théoret,

## OBJECT
### GREEN WOODEN MASK
*by Diane Williams*

FEATURES:
* Chin-strap beard
* Mustache
* Scalloped hairline

Somebody, who?—saw fit to make this mustachioed, green-painted, wooden mask, with a black scalloped hairline, and a Pinocchio nose.

The tip of its nose is chipped and I tried out a crude restoration. I dabbed some green paint on it.

A black beard has been applied, not by me, under the chin, and the beard shows up also upon its jowls.

The mask is undersized enough for a child to wear. But which child where and when could ever have been asked or forced to wear it, and why?

I tried it out (not pleasant to do), just to see if it fits *my* little head, but no.

The mysterious mask is most wonderful to meet up with, nevertheless, when I see it, which is often. It is on my wall.

Here is an evergreen face whose expression is earnest, I think, or sincere—a reassuring spirit—a small one, yes—and he has been magnanimous. ✶

Lise Tremblay, Delisle. In translating French texts into English—"that dominatrix," as you call it in *Permanent Revolution*—how did you avoid alienating their cultural difference?

GS: Certainly there's never a complete transition from one space to another. Essentially I grew up with Franco-Canadian culture and language from about the age of eight. It's not as if I were translating Podolski from Euro-French. These translations with Quebecois writers were very collaborative. I would write a few pages, and then we would sit down and have a drink—that always helps.

BLVR: I wish we could have one now. I'm sorry we're on Zoom.

GS: Well, it's five o'clock somewhere. But, you know, France [Théoret] particularly—as you can see from reading the "Virginia and Colette" essay—was really my beacon, as I was hers, for many years. Our relationship was so intense. So it wasn't hard for me to translate these people, but it would be hard for me to translate people coming from another place. Even New York or Paris is more difficult.

BLVR: Is writing instrumental for life, or conversely?

GS: I can't really separate the two. I think about language all the time. An hour doesn't go by that I'm not thinking about writing. Not even an hour. And speaking of pleasure, this is it. ✶

*Illustration by Kristian Hammerstad*

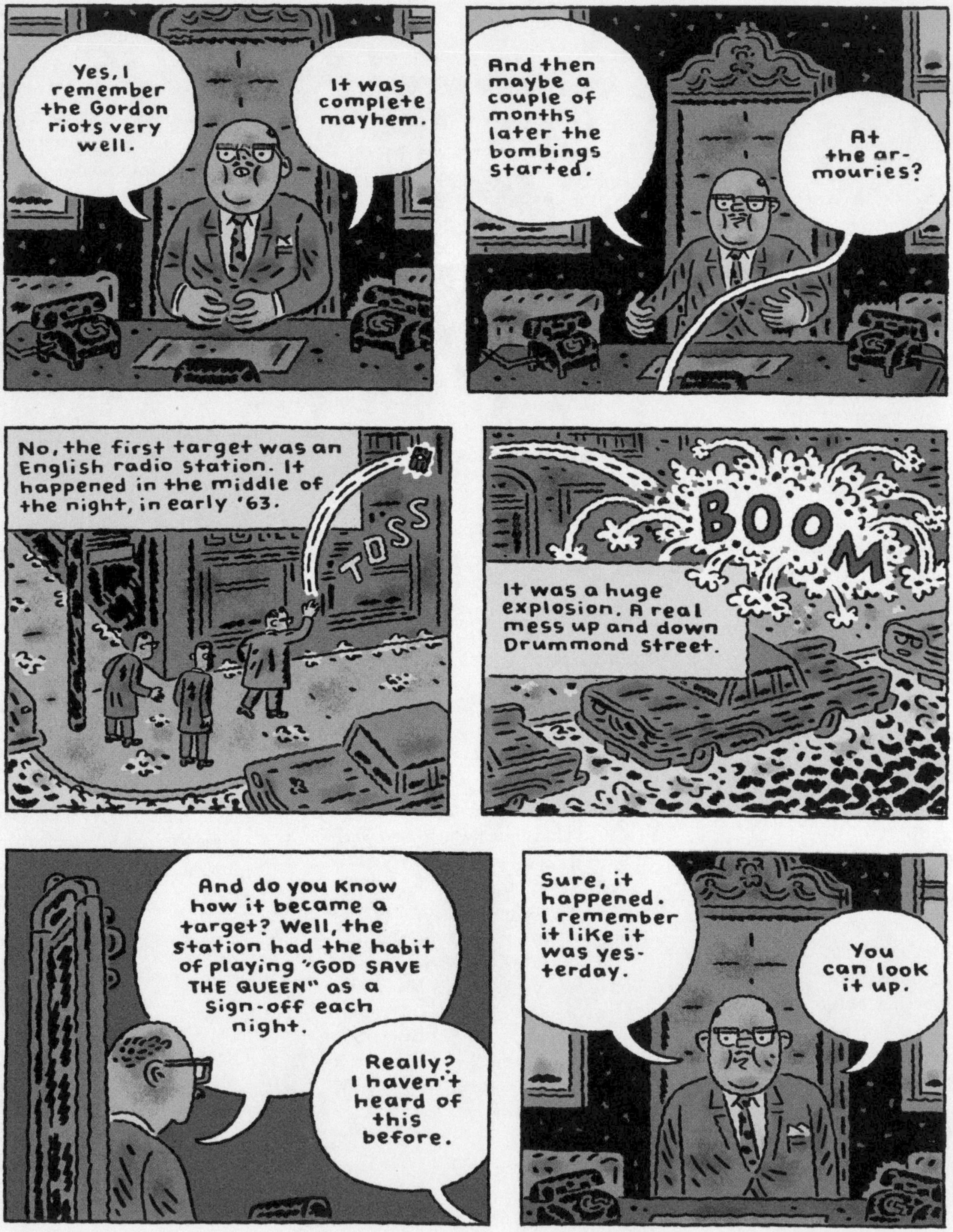
Yes, I remember the Gordon riots very well.
It was complete mayhem.
And then maybe a couple of months later the bombings started.
At the armouries?
No, the first target was an English radio station. It happened in the middle of the night, in early '63.
TOSS
BOOM
It was a huge explosion. A real mess up and down Drummond street.
And do you know how it became a target? Well, the station had the habit of playing "GOD SAVE THE QUEEN" as a sign-off each night.
Really? I haven't heard of this before.
Sure, it happened. I remember it like it was yesterday.
You can look it up.

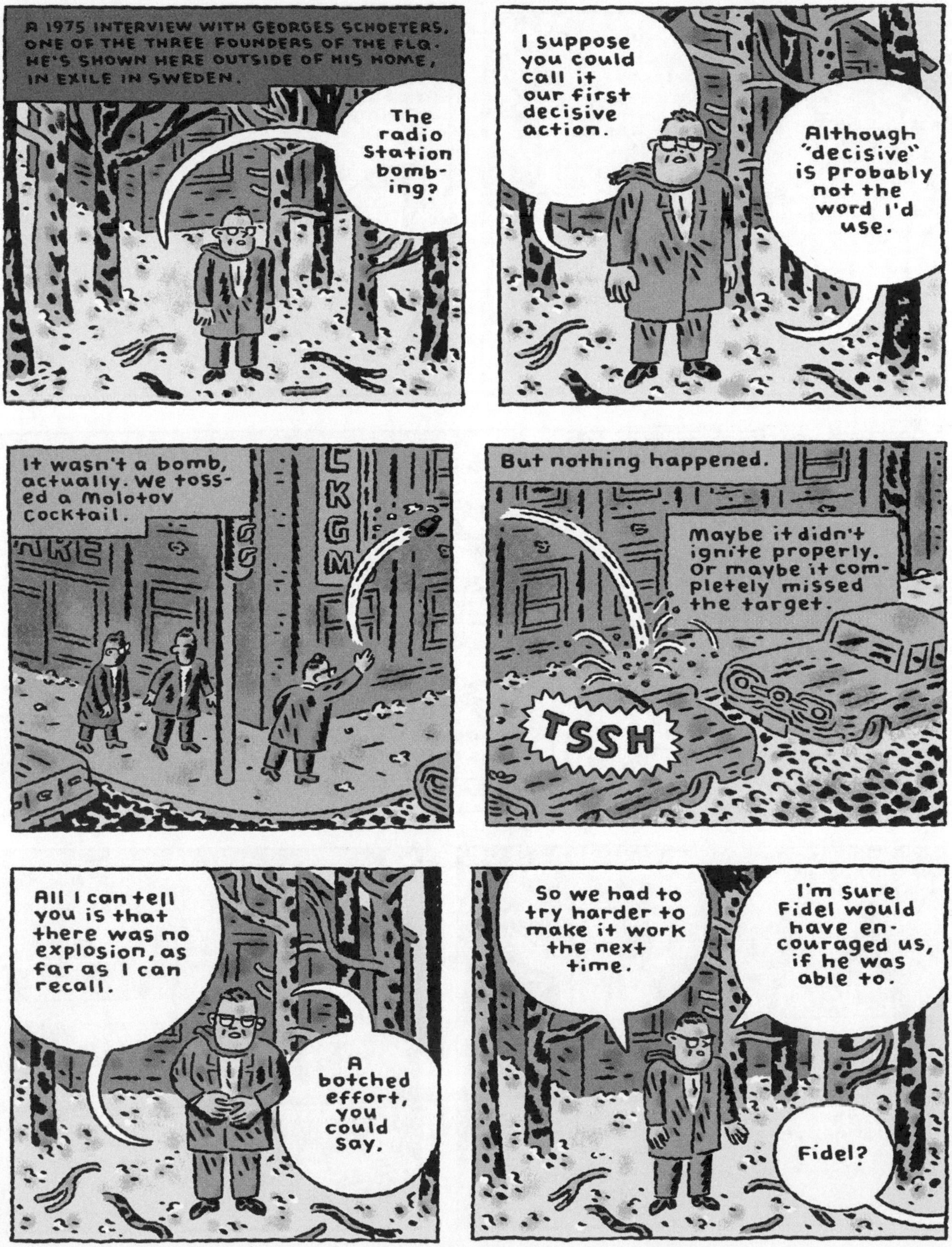
A 1975 INTERVIEW WITH GEORGES SCHOETERS, ONE OF THE THREE FOUNDERS OF THE FLQ. HE'S SHOWN HERE OUTSIDE OF HIS HOME, IN EXILE IN SWEDEN.
The radio station bombing?
I suppose you could call it our first decisive action.
Although "decisive" is probably not the word I'd use.
It wasn't a bomb, actually. We tossed a Molotov cocktail.
CKGM
But nothing happened.
Maybe it didn't ignite properly. Or maybe it completely missed the target.
TSSH
All I can tell you is that there was no explosion, as far as I can recall.
A botched effort, you could say.
So we had to try harder to make it work the next time.
I'm sure Fidel would have encouraged us, if he was able to.
Fidel?

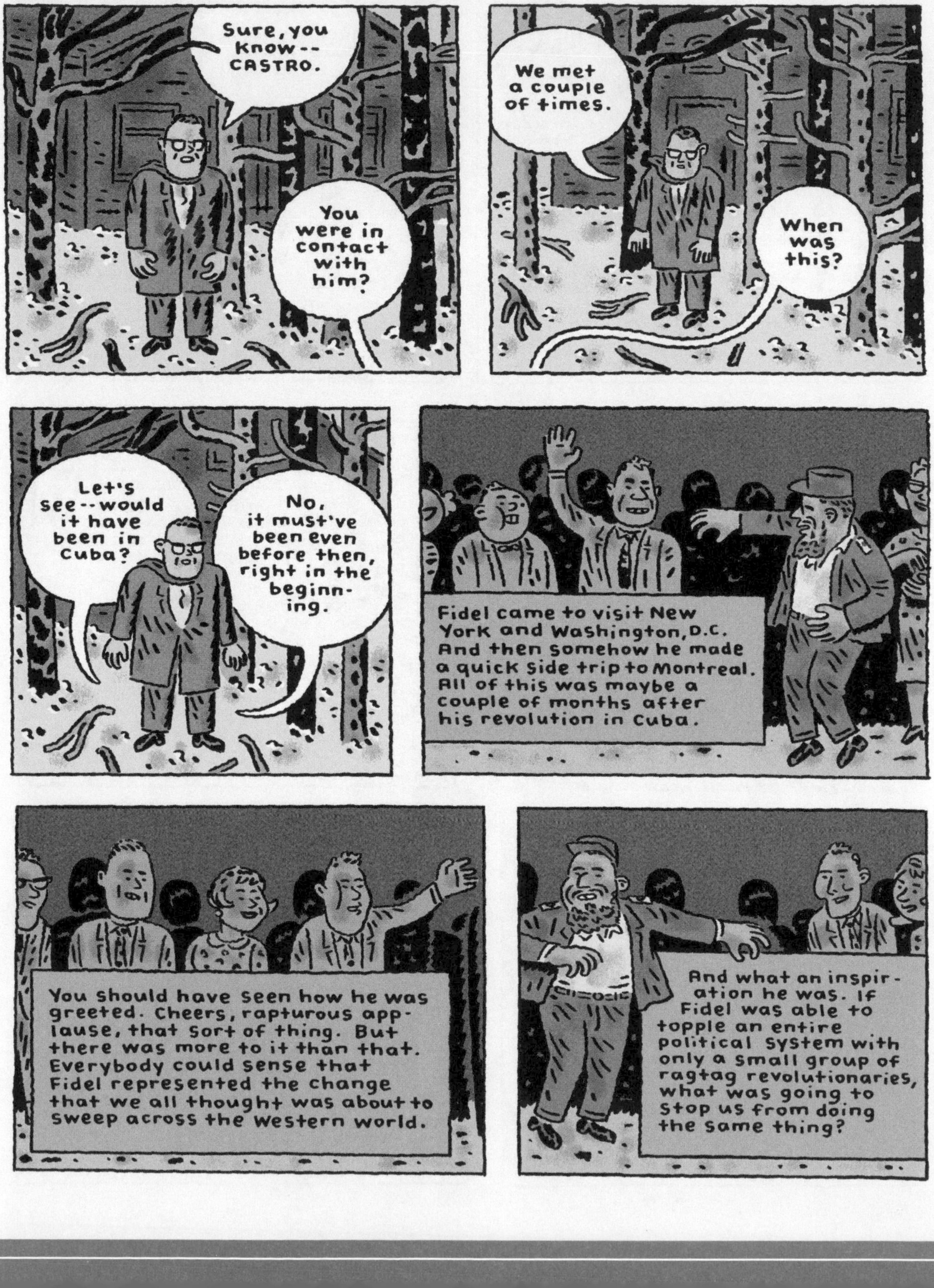
Sure, you know-- CASTRO.
You were in contact with him?
We met a couple of times.
When was this?
Let's see--would it have been in Cuba?
No, it must've been even before then, right in the beginn-ing.
Fidel came to visit New York and Washington, D.C. And then somehow he made a quick side trip to Montreal. All of this was maybe a couple of months after his revolution in Cuba.
You should have seen how he was greeted. Cheers, rapturous app-lause, that sort of thing. But there was more to it than that. Everybody could sense that Fidel represented the change that we all thought was about to sweep across the Western world.
And what an inspir-ation he was. If Fidel was able to topple an entire political system with only a small group of ragtag revolutionaries, what was going to stop us from doing the same thing?

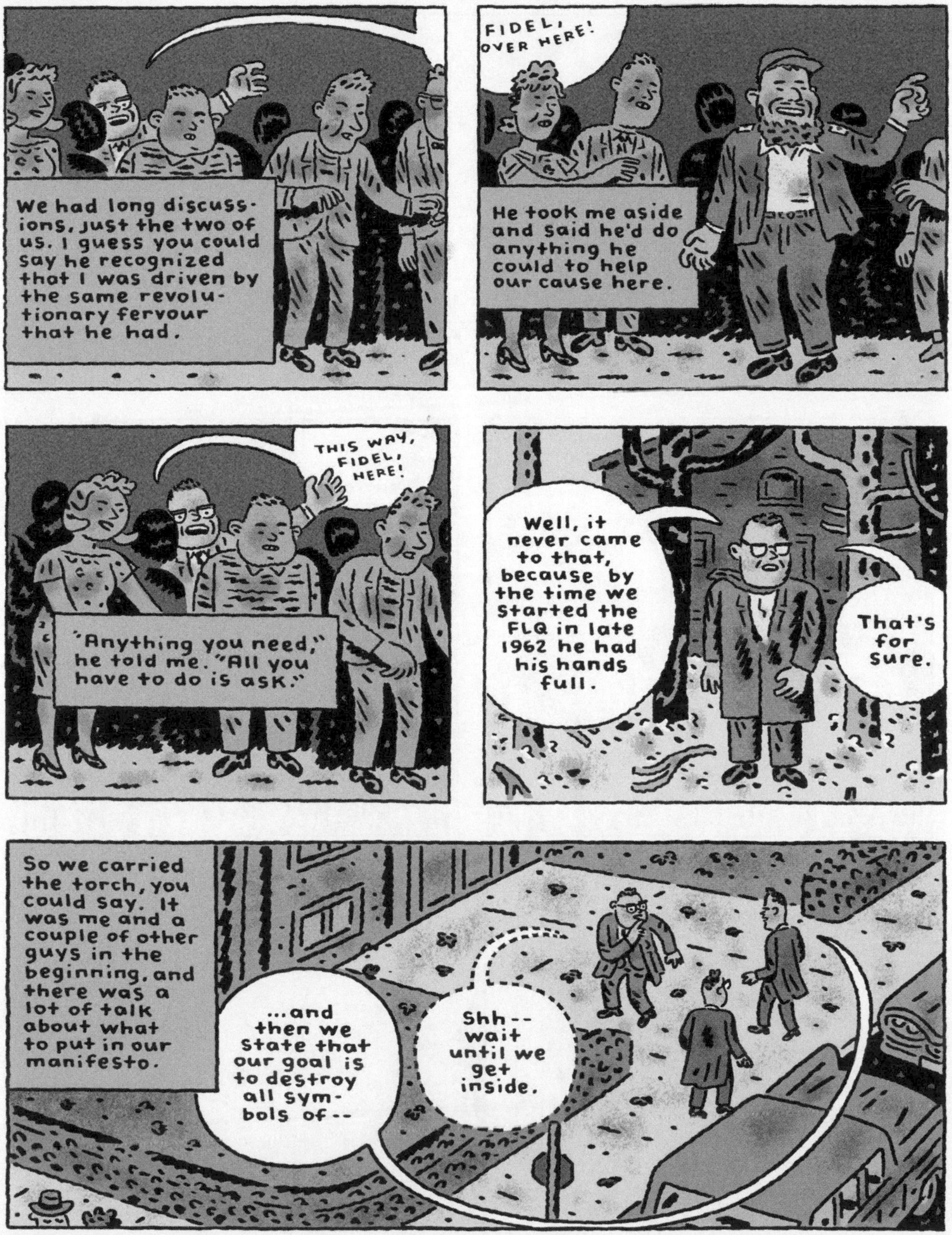
We had long discussions, just the two of us. I guess you could say he recognized that I was driven by the same revolutionary fervour that he had.
FIDEL, OVER HERE!
He took me aside and said he'd do anything he could to help our cause here.
THIS WAY, FIDEL, HERE!
"Anything you need," he told me. "All you have to do is ask."
Well, it never came to that, because by the time we started the FLQ in late 1962 he had his hands full.
That's for sure.
So we carried the torch, you could say. It was me and a couple of other guys in the beginning, and there was a lot of talk about what to put in our manifesto.
...and then we state that our goal is to destroy all symbols of--
Shh--wait until we get inside.

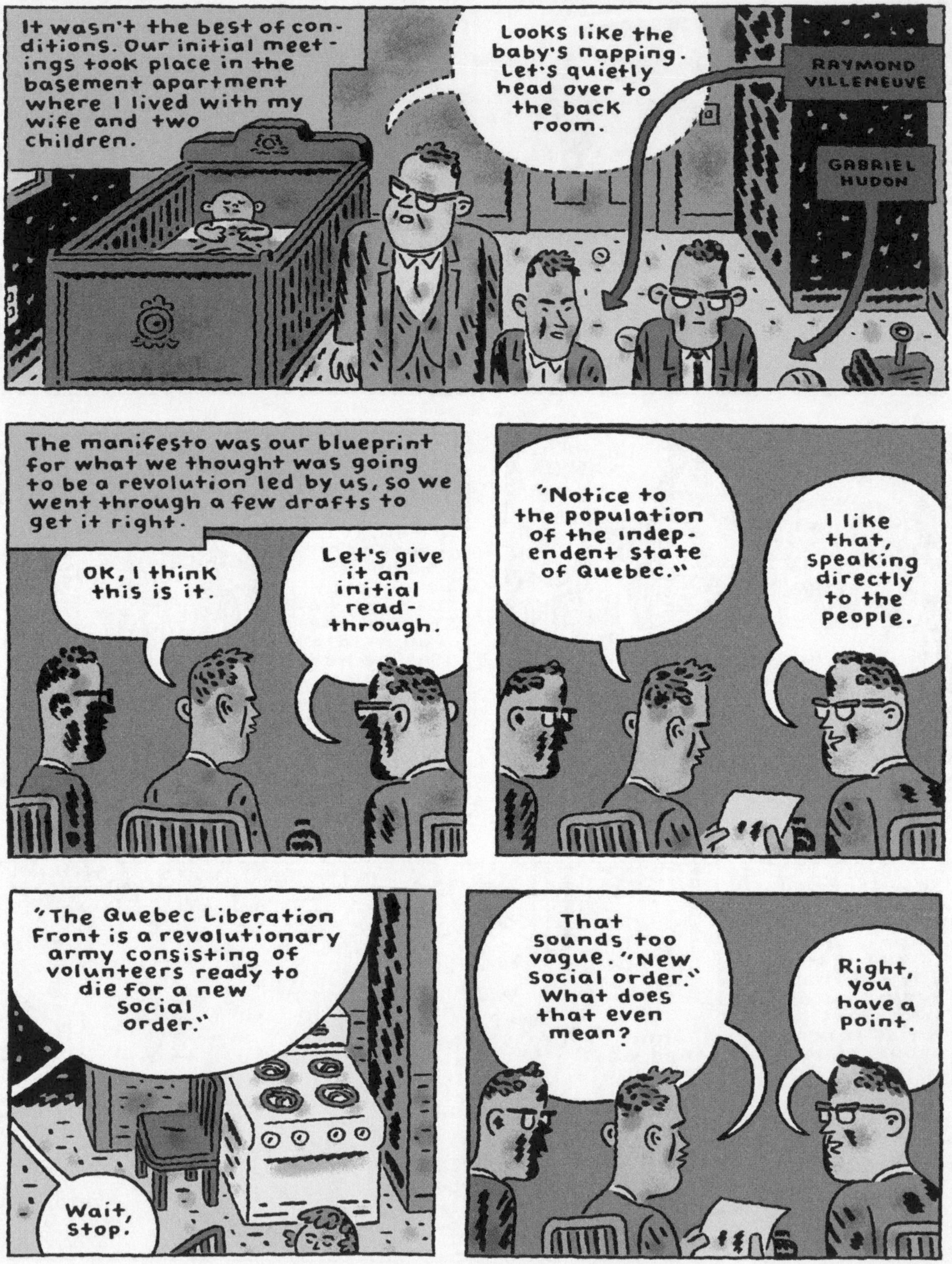
It wasn't the best of conditions. Our initial meetings took place in the basement apartment where I lived with my wife and two children.
Looks like the baby's napping. Let's quietly head over to the back room.
RAYMOND VILLENEUVE
GABRIEL HUDON
The manifesto was our blueprint for what we thought was going to be a revolution led by us, so we went through a few drafts to get it right.
OK, I think this is it.
Let's give it an initial read-through.
"Notice to the population of the independent State of Quebec."
I like that, speaking directly to the people.
"The Quebec Liberation Front is a revolutionary army consisting of volunteers ready to die for a new social order."
Wait, stop.
That sounds too vague. "New social order." What does that even mean?
Right, you have a point.

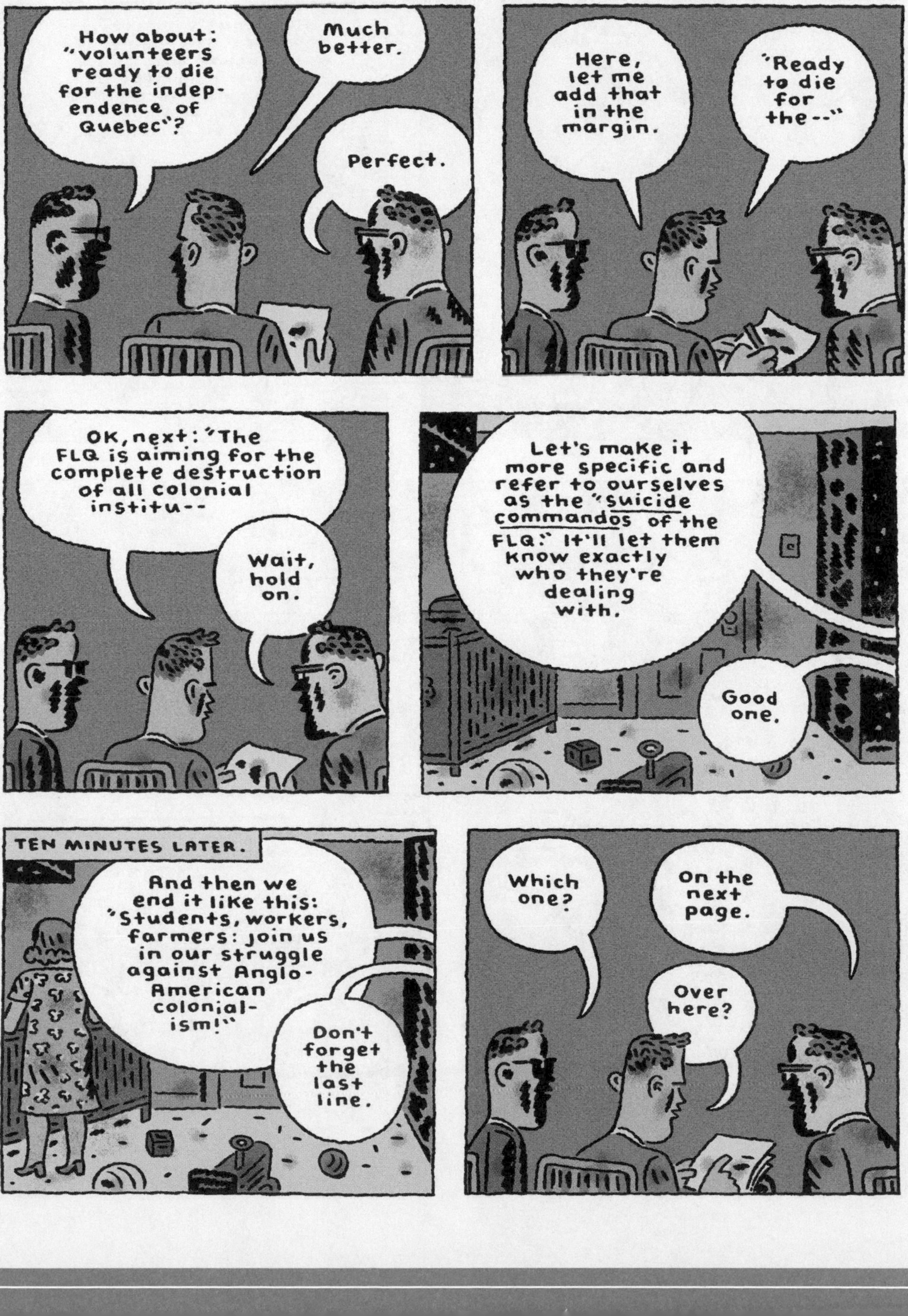
How about: "volunteers ready to die for the independence of Quebec"?
Much better.
Perfect.
Here, let me add that in the margin.
"Ready to die for the--"
OK, next: "The FLQ is aiming for the complete destruction of all colonial institu--
Wait, hold on.
Let's make it more specific and refer to ourselves as the "suicide commandos of the FLQ." It'll let them know exactly who they're dealing with.
Good one.
TEN MINUTES LATER.
And then we end it like this: "Students, workers, farmers: join us in our struggle against Anglo-American colonialism!"
Don't forget the last line.
Which one?
On the next page.
Over here?

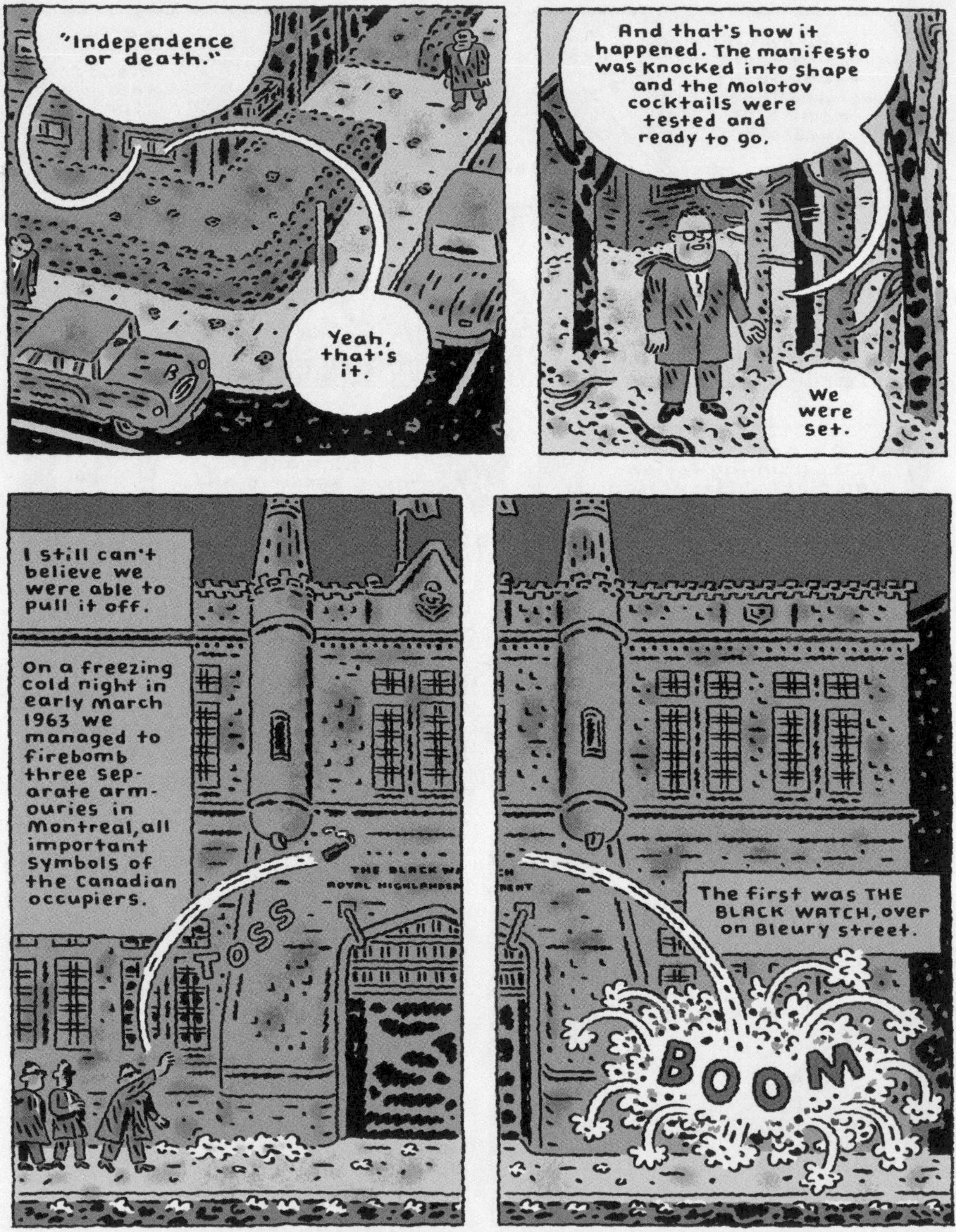
"Independence or death."
Yeah, that's it.
And that's how it happened. The manifesto was knocked into shape and the Molotov cocktails were tested and ready to go.
We were set.
I still can't believe we were able to pull it off.
On a freezing cold night in early March 1963 we managed to firebomb three separate armouries in Montreal, all important symbols of the Canadian occupiers.
TOSS
The first was THE BLACK WATCH, over on Bleury street.
BOOM

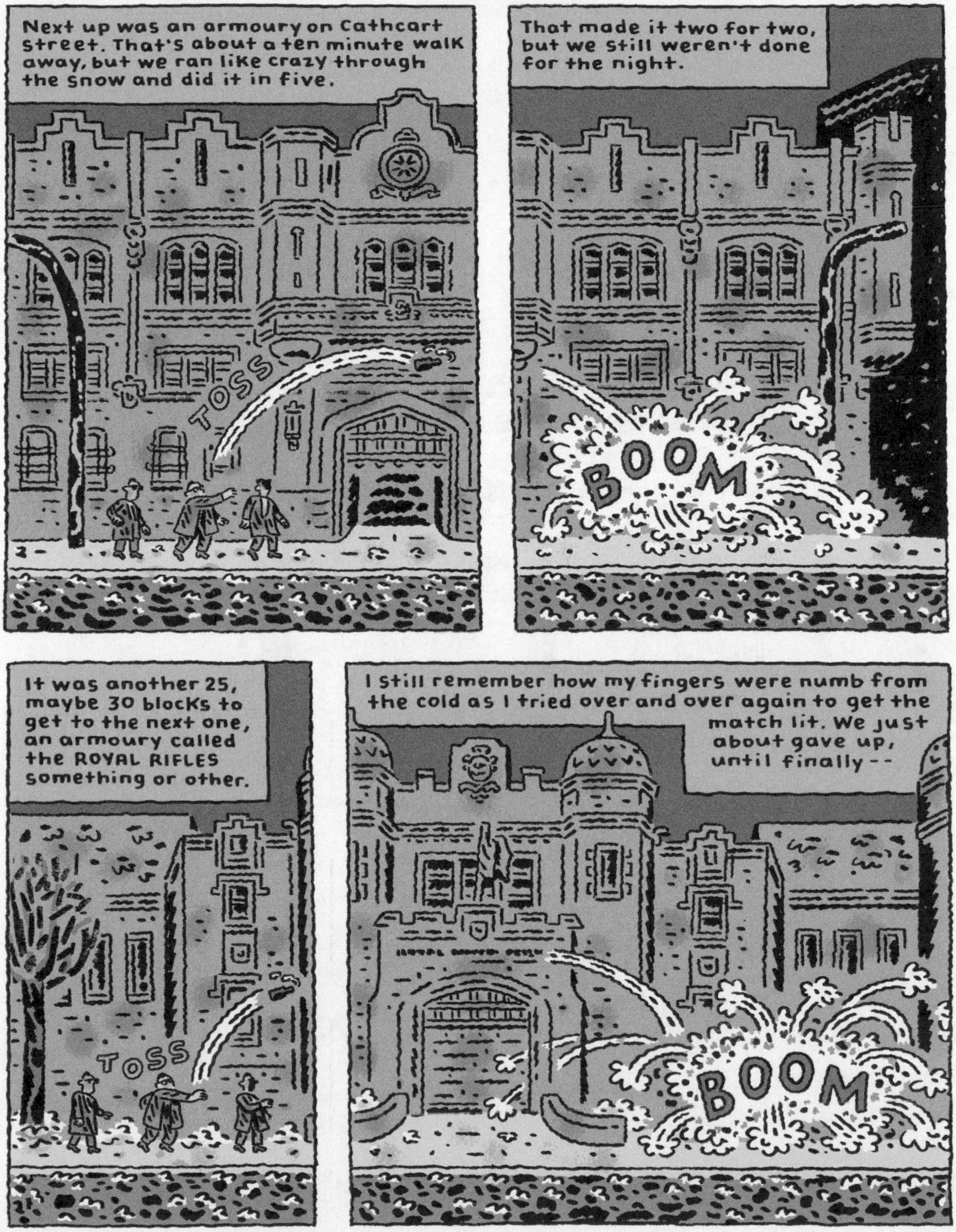
Next up was an armoury on Cathcart Street. That's about a ten minute walk away, but we ran like crazy through the snow and did it in five.
TOSS
That made it two for two, but we still weren't done for the night.
BOOM
It was another 25, maybe 30 blocks to get to the next one, an armoury called the ROYAL RIFLES something or other.
TOSS
I still remember how my fingers were numb from the cold as I tried over and over again to get the match lit. We just about gave up, until finally--
BOOM

# Explore the world from up close.

## ORION
NATURE AND CULTURE

*Subscribe to America's finest environmental magazine.*

# WILLIAM KENTRIDGE

[ARTIST]

"OLD QUESTIONS DON'T DISAPPEAR."

Objects found in various William Kentridge installations:
*Director's chairs*
*Shipping crates*
*A studio replica*
*Singer sewing machines*
*A large wooden-ribbed breathing machine (also known as "The Elephant")*

**W**illiam Kentridge's first New York solo show, Drawings for Projection (1998), radically changed my way of thinking about drawing, film, history, and time. His analog hand-drawn animations mesmerize and haunt. Kentridge's storytelling process is generative, generous, and expansive. Although my first encounter with Kentridge's work was through his drawings and films, over the course of his career he has worked across multiple mediums, including printmaking, sculpture, theater, opera, and installation. Regardless of the medium, his work is capacious and collaborative. It can be at once seriously dark and seriously humorous. It often circles historic traumas, particularly the harsh South African political landscape, but his subject is really humanity writ large.

On November 15, 2022, I interviewed Kentridge at The Broad, a museum in downtown Los Angeles, where his show In Praise of Shadows had just opened. The

*Illustration by Kristian Hammerstad*

*career-spanning exhibition features drawings, sculptures, prints, tapestries, films, and film installations.*

*Entering the show, I step into a room with a bronze sculpture that looks like a vintage movie-recording device. The sculpture,* Action *(2018), is a newer work, while the other pieces—drawings depicting golden-age Hollywood icons such as Marlene Dietrich, Humphrey Bogart, Greta Garbo, and Groucho Marx—are works Kentridge made during the beginning of his career, when he was working in the South African film industry. The curator of* In Praise of Shadows, *Ed Schad, has drawn a convincing through line from Kentridge's work to the movie industry of Los Angeles.*

*I interview Kentridge in a room with chartreuse curtains. We sit on what feels like a stage. I am wearing a mustard-yellow suit and Kentridge is wearing his usual black artist ensemble (but without his signature fedora). It feels like we are both actors without an audience. Later that evening, after the interview, we transform into audience members at the packed REDCAT theater to watch the North American premiere of Kentridge's play* Houseboy, *which traffics in the effects of French colonialism. During the play, the room is tense and alive. The twelve actors speak directly to us.*

*—Natasha Boas*

### I. "THE WORLD IS LEAKING"

THE BELIEVER: So much of the work you do is from the perspective of a South African who was raised in apartheid-era Johannesburg, where you have continued to live throughout your life. Your father, Sir Sydney Kentridge, was the lawyer of Archbishop Desmond Tutu and Nelson Mandela. We've heard your remarkable life story before.

WILLIAM KENTRIDGE: Yes, we've heard this story too many times.

BLVR: In what ways have your preoccupations shifted over time? What are the new areas you want to explore? What are the new nervous systems in which you are working? Or is your work interested in the repetition of the same themes?

WK: That is a very good and hard question. It would be lovely not to be going back into repetition. But we know from psychoanalysis that repetition is hard to avoid until you work out what it is that's being repeated. The big questions shift and change, but they're still fundamental. How does one find emancipation? What is the best one can hope for in the world as it is? There was the belief we all had twenty years ago that rationality and enlightenment were what we were heading toward, and that countries like South Africa needed to be pushed out of their oppressive systems into the world. But what the last fifteen years have shown us is how precarious that idea actually is. What we assumed everyone was moving toward, a liberal democracy, actually is not a liberal democracy. And even in the United States, where it seemed unchallengeable, suddenly democracy is quite precarious. Not just because people stormed the Capitol in that chaotic way. No, much more dangerously, because the actual lawmakers and judges are the real threat, rather than the hooligans.

BLVR: The threat to democracy has become part of the establishment.

WK: Old questions don't disappear. In some ways they become much more immediate. Questions around the relationship of emancipation to violence or certainty are urgent.

I started work on a theater project in January, and I know a lot about the language of it; I know the cardboard masks we use; I know the kind of megaphones and piano, and the kind of bellowing into the megaphones, and the piece by Schubert being played. I have a sense of someone falling asleep continuously on the piano. I know there's a chorus of women picking up the pieces, whether it's local pieces or, metaphorically, the world. So the anxiety that this project responds to feels close and certain. What I don't know are the specifics. Which particular story are we telling? And is it enough to just start with the broad question? If one had to give the project a phrase, I would say, "The world is leaking" or "The world is falling apart, the dead report for duty, and it's always the women that pick up the pieces."

BLVR: Your theater project sounds like a story about women's work. It sounds like the phrase "A woman's work is never done."

WK: Yes. Is that enough of a basis to go on? Or is it too vague? Does it need a particular story about the trade in body parts? What are all the disasters in the world now? What are the ways they can be represented? Right now the project is caught between wanting to do something that can encompass very wide things, and the feeling that for it to work, we also have to be very specific. It's very specific in terms of medium. And it's not yet specific in terms of narrative. So there's the edge of a new nervous system.

BLVR: Intriguing.

WK: But it isn't a basis for a novel.

BLVR: You always talk about being compelled to draw, and say that drawing is its own ontology and that it coincides with the timing of thinking. I'm thinking about the stories you want to tell and your relationship to storytelling, whether that is something that is grounded in a South African or an African history. Are you an African artist? Are you a South African artist? Are you just an artist?

WK: OK. They showed some of my work in the African section of the Metropolitan Museum [of Art]. I said, "Why am I being shown there?" "Well," they said, "not just because you're an artist from Africa." They said, "So much of your work is applied art. Its images are made in the service of a performance, in the service of a ritual." The drawing is made in the service of the film. The film is made in the service of a piece of theater.

BLVR: That's one way of defining "African art" as a whole.

WK: It makes sense to me. I think, yes, my art is South African. African artists with a polemic understand that the history and weight of Europe are also part of Africa. To extract Europe from Africa, and to try to find an essential African purity, is a false activity that can only lead to a false result.

## II. THE STUDIO AS SUBJECT

BLVR: How did you respond to the initial COVID lockdown?

WK: I had a fantastic eighteen months in my studio.

BLVR: It seems like many artists felt this way—relieved that we could do our work and not have to spend all our time traveling and socializing.

WK: We all had COVID a couple of times in the studio, but we all got through it. And I spent the time making a series of films about what happens in the studio—nine half-hour films.

BLVR: Does the studio practice become your subject?

WK: The subject was what happened in the space, and it becomes the subject on which different things are predicated. But it also becomes the claustrophobic enclosed space you never leave. So I was also locked down in that sense. So that's been the big project we're just finishing now.

BLVR: You talk about the studio almost as if it were a character.

WK: It is a kind of character. In these films, we film at night, when the camera and the sousaphone have their own life going on in the studio. The objects have their own life.

BLVR: Are these films being show here at The Broad?

WK: No, they're not. We're still finishing them. We have to try to find a place to distribute them. If it's animation, it's fine, easy to put in galleries—we just show them. But this longer form needs a more traditional projection-room situation.

BLVR: Have you never had a feature film project? Or a fantasy of one?

WK: There are offers and I am tempted. Everybody who goes to the movies has dreams of making a feature-length film. But I would be a very different director if I did. There's a language of film directing that is very different from [that of] theatrical directing. And I realize that's where my director experience is—in theater. The actor is already me.

BLVR: I think about this in terms of auto-fiction. I'm kind of obsessed with the arguments around auto-fiction. Is it fiction? Is it memoir? I guess you make auto-portraits using yourself, or a kind of self-portrait. But what else is going on?

WK: What else is going on with that? In the films I made during COVID, all the dialogue is me, and I dialogue with myself. There are two of me having conversations. It's not

*All images from William Kentridge,* In Praise of Shadows, *The Broad, Los Angeles, November 12, 2022–April 9, 2023. This page:* Double Vision. *© 2007 by William Kentridge. Stereoscopic card (from a set of eight) with stereopticon. Courtesy of the artist;* Underweysung der Messung: Melencolia, Momento Mori, Still Life, A Cat in the Meat Trade, Étant Donnée, Larder. *© 2007 by William Kentridge. Set of six stereoscopic photogravures with stereoscope. Courtesy of the artist;* Less Brocade on the Jacket. *© 2015 by William Kentridge. Ink on found pages. Courtesy of the artist and Marian Goodman Gallery, New York;* Rebus. *© 2013 by William Kentridge. Bronze, suite of nine sculpture (from an edition of twelve). Courtesy of private collection;* And When He Returned. *© 2019 by William Kentridge. Tapestry weave with embroidery. Warp: polyester. Weft and embroidery: mohair, acrylic, and polyester. Courtesy of the artist;* Drawing for Studio Life (Landscape after Tinus de Jongh). *© 2020 by William Kentridge. Charcoal, pastel, and red pencil on paper. Courtesy of private collection.*

a documentary, like: let's have two talking heads interview each other. It's all the different conversations that one has with oneself in one's head. And as the film went on, that was just one small element of the story. But as the editing happened, the films got shorter, but those conversations stayed key to it. I think the hope was that it would turn into a real interrogation.

BLVR: What is "a real interrogation"?

WK: A real interrogation would be asking me questions I didn't know the answers to, and then me discovering answers I hadn't expected. I'm not aware of it having gone into that different realm. So all the things I say are right. I mean, they are. It's a mixture of things about the work and things about myself. The series is now called *Self-Portrait as a Coffee Pot.*

BLVR: We see the coffee pot in some of the work already as an animate and an inanimate object.

WK: I think I am saying that you can create a biography by describing the objects around something or someone.

BLVR: The objects tell the story.

WK: For example, by the books. The books on your bookshelf are a kind of portrait of you by what you've collected, everything you've read. All the drawings you've done of your life are a kind of self-portrait.

BLVR: So this new body of work that you're talking about is actually going much more into autobiography?

WK: Yes.

BLVR: You are so prolific. Have you ever had a moment when you have been compelled to not mark-make?

WK: When I travel, I don't feel a compulsion. Some artists draw every day, and I really don't, but I'm missing not being in the studio all the time. I'll feel much happier when I'm back to drawing.

BLVR: Is the studio the only place you make things?

WK: It is. I trust the studio. When I'm in the studio—actually physically cutting, drawing—ideas come in through that process.

### III. NO SUCH THING AS CLEAN

BLVR: The curator of *In Praise of Shadows* conceived of the exhibition as a conversation between California and South Africa. I do think many of the images make that connection, from the direct references to Hollywood actors and the film apparatus to the Gold Rush and mining exploitation. And there are the trees and the many themes around the trouble with certain monuments. This is your first show in Los Angeles in twenty years. Do you think your work reads differently now? Here at The Broad, they've created a whole series of public programs for you, and it's all with African American scholars.

WK: It's interesting.

BLVR: Will you have read up on your abolitionist contemporary theory before you get to Berkeley for your performance there in March?

WK: I had supper on Monday with Claudia Rankine and Patrisse Cullors, a cofounder of the Black Lives Matter Global Network Foundation.

BLVR: You are very up-to-date, then, of course.

WK: I did the conversation with Claudia as a public program for the show here at The Broad during the opening weekend. The conversation was titled "The Un-Private Collection."

BLVR: I am quoting the description of the talk from the museum's website: "Both Kentridge and Rankine examine symbols and monuments as they appear in our respective societies, rooting out colonial and racist structures—Kentridge from the vantage point of a white South African of privileged background, and Rankine from the vantage point [of] a Black woman in the United States."

WK: I admit I was a little bit anxious before the conversation with Claudia.

BLVR: I would imagine.

WK: Rankine has taught my work for some years. She is very interested in my Centre for the Less Good Idea, my experimental center in Johannesburg. It was a very friendly conversation. There were a lot of questions that no one else had asked. For me, abolitionism is a bit like the situation in South Africa, which I always described not as a post-apartheid society, but as a post-anti-apartheid society. In other words, the interest of the whole world in the anti-apartheid movement had its moment. But it doesn't mean that the traces—and, more than the traces, the presence of the results of apartheid—are not still in the country. So that's an easy starting point.

Being white in South Africa means you understand from the beginning that you are compromised and complicit and part of it. And to try to say, *I'm clean. I'm a clean South African?* You are not. It's not possible. You start from accepting an impurity. And you go from there.

BLVR: Johannesburg and LA also have similarities in terms of their urban sprawl and exurbs. I still have a sense of museums as being places where you can go and discover other parts of the world that aren't yours.

WK: When I did the exhibition in China, I decided I wanted to do one piece that was very much concerned with questioning: What is my relationship to China? What is it? Who is it? When I did a piece in Berlin, it was very much: What is Germany to South Africa? And that became the genocide in Namibia. The one in China was about the Cultural Revolution. The piece in Turkey was about Trotsky and his exile in Istanbul.

BLVR: You always think of the context.

WK: They were specific projects. This show was a specific project. In London, there were a lot of tapestries made specifically for it and installations tailored around it. Here in LA, it's much more from the existing body of work and from the things that are already in The Broad collection.

BLVR: I was riveted by one piece in this show, *The Refusal of Time* (2012)—an immersive, unwieldy thirty-minute, five-channel video installation. It feels like a workshop, or a lab, and it is really hard to understand, but I love that I don't understand it. There is a large wooden-ribbed device that sits at the heart of the space, like a breathing machine, that opens and closes in rhythm with asynchronous images and sounds. It's crazy and beautiful.

WK: Thank you.

BLVR: These bric-a-brac built environments continue throughout the show. It sometimes feels like you're walking through a movie set or hanging out in a studio. In one installation you even have director's chairs set up that we can sit on. It's in the nine-channel video installation *7 Fragments for Georges Méliès* (2003) that you pay tribute to Méliès, the pioneering French filmmaker.

WK: Yes, this is all intentional. The designer of the show is Sabine Theunissen, who also creates theater sets for many of my projects. She is reproducing the agency of making—whether it is the making of films or the mise-en-scène of the actual exhibition, the materiality is there. Also, a filmmaker like Méliès was more of a stage magician and was interested in the performances of transformation. Méliès would perform in front of his drawings.

BLVR: I am also thinking of another piece: a charcoal, pastel, and gouache on paper. It's a kind of selfie. You're looking in the rearview mirror and—

WK: You see my eyes.

BLVR: Is that the one? The drawing?

WK: The film.

BLVR: No, I am thinking of a drawing downstairs.

WK: The drawing. Right.

BLVR: It affected me.

WK: Was it the rearview mirror one?

BLVR: You use mirroring a lot. I remember now: it's called *Flood at the Opera* [1986].

WK: Sitting in the car, driving through the city, do you see your eyes in the mirror?

BLVR: I see your eyes in the mirror. It makes me think of California car culture. Like Johannesburg, LA is a driving suburban city. It's like you are taking a selfie in your car. It's an "auto" auto-portrait. Literally.

### IV. HALF-HEARD CONVERSATIONS

BLVR: When you discuss enlightenment, you talk about how the enlightenment metaphor is the backbone of colonialism. You show the underbelly of it in a lot of your work. Why does your work resonate in so many different historical, national, and political contexts?

WK: I discussed this when we did the play *Ubu and the Truth Commission*, which was made from archival text of the testimony given at the Truth and Reconciliation Commission mixed together with Alfred Jarry's *Ubu [the King]*.

BLVR: Yes, I'm familiar with the play.

WK: We did the play in South Africa knowing it would be seen in South Africa and would make sense. But people said, "OK, it makes sense here, but how is it going to make any sense outside of South Africa?" It's so specific and so local. The first place outside we took it to was when it was shown in Weimar at a festival there, where people said, "This is so fantastic. This is about us, this is about reparations and our unspoken history in the East, which is Gauteng."

BLVR: Because it was about repression?

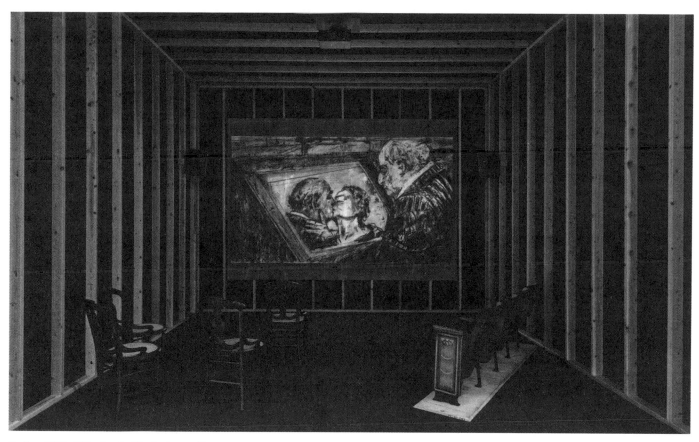

*City Deep. ©2020 by William Kentridge. HD video. Courtesy of the artist.*

WK: We thought it wouldn't make sense outside of South Africa, but it did. Then we took it to Zurich, where they said, "This is all about us. It's about German money, Jewish money, and Nazi money. This happened here." And in France they asked, "Is this is about the French resistance or is this about collaboration?"

BLVR: Everybody sees themselves.

WK: And then somebody said, "I saw this play. I'm from Romania, and I know this play is about Romania. It's a local play about Romania." So I think even though the specifics were not completely understood by all audiences, and perhaps even though each audience member did not know exactly what each image represented, there was a sense of it being located in a local way, which made it resonate very far, in a lot of very disparate places around the world. I don't think

this is generosity. I think it's that we can't stop ourselves from making those connections. We're constantly testing our understanding of what we are seeing. There are so many commonalities around the world that it's not so strange for something to resonate.

BLVR: This is why people are so moved by your work. One of your pieces may address apartheid, but something about it also resonates with a person who lives in the American Midwest. I won't say your work is universal, because *universal* is a word that hearkens back to the Enlightenment. I'll say that your work is human. It is capacious. Your work is of the human experience.

WK: *Universal* implies that in all circumstances the questions will be identical and nothing will ever change. There is a stasis implied in the term *universal*.

Singer Trio. © 2019 by William Kentridge. Singer sewing machines, four breast drills, antique wooden rulers, mild steel, aluminum, wood, electronics. Courtesy of Goodman Gallery, South Africa; Let Us Enter the Chapter (diptych). © 2013 by William Kentridge. India ink, charcoal, and pastel, digital print on Shorter Oxford Dictionary paper tabbed to Velin Arches 400 gsm. Courtesy of private collection.

BLVR: Right. In the term *universal* there is no room for movement or radical change.

WK: There are so many points of connection in different contexts that we live by and need to live by and are nourished by.

BLVR: Right. So maybe *nourishing* is the adjective I'm looking for to define your work?

WK: My work is about having read *Ulysses* and never having been to Dublin. And it's about my imagination of Dublin's bay and the beaches.

BLVR: Exactly.

WK: It's a mixture of my memories.

BLVR: Is it fantasy?

WK: It's my memory of different beaches, and words or phrases that jump out while I'm reading.

BLVR: Is it imagining?

WK: Just because I haven't been to Dublin, that doesn't stop me from connecting to the book. I have a different connection to the book than someone who's lived all their life in Dublin, but I still have my connection. The most interesting use of one tradition is always made by people from outside the given tradition.

BLVR: Thank goodness for outsider perspectives.

WK: Mistranslation and misunderstanding are vital.

BLVR: Exactly. I completely agree. That's why I think the process of making a translation, or the mistakes in a transcription, are always the most interesting.

WK: Yes.

BLVR: And revealing.

WK: Absolutely. It's also when you can't quite understand something that you're most actively imagining what it could be. You can feel the energy of trying to interpret.

BLVR: The overwriting or the meta-work.

WK: I love conversations I can only half hear.

BLVR: I recently went to a dinner party in a restaurant that was so loud that no one could understand what the other person was saying, and not only was it hilarious, it was totally meta. We could have used a Leonora Carrington hearing trumpet. We ended up understanding new things from all our misunderstandings.

WK: Those instances are exhilarating because you're so busy filling in words that you haven't heard, jumping across gaps.

BLVR: The fragments making the phrases. It's like what you

say about shadows. When you see a shadow, you understand that you're seeing a very limited part of an object and you have to fill in the rest yourself. You immediately become complicit in making the meaning.

### V. THE CROCODILE

BLVR: Is there any medium you would like to work in that you haven't?

WK: Yes, but collaboration is difficult. In most cases I just look around my studio and realize that my studio already has it all.

BLVR: Right. No need to find the best marble or whatever.

WK: Most often I am able, for example, to find a foundry that has certain capacities and then ask: What are the things we can make together?

BLVR: Right. The constraints help make the project.

WK: And working very closely with the foundry workers helps make the project. When working with a costume designer, I think, What are the kinds of puppets that will come from our conversation? It's never, *Here is my idea. Please execute it*. It's never, *Here is my idea for a drawing. Please find someone to make it*.

BLVR: Your conversations sound very different from what Frank Gehry's were with me when I was a young sculptor. He just sent me a picture of a crocodile and said, "Please turn this crocodile into a chandelier." Then the crocodile chandelier ended up at Rebecca's, a nouveau Mexican fantasy-themed restaurant he designed, and later, I think, went to auction at Sotheby's, and is now in the Broads' family home. Did you see it?

WK: Yes! I saw your crocodile. I thought it was a fish.

### VI. TWO ACTORS DOWN

BLVR: Tonight I will be at your performance of *Houseboy* at the REDCAT

theater. You developed the play at your Centre for the Less Good Idea in Johannesburg. I read that it's based on the 1956 novel by Cameroonian diplomat Ferdinand Oyono, and that it deals with French colonialism in Cameroon.

WK: Yes. It's wonderful that you will be there.

BLVR: I am sure we'll find more of your themes of historical participation and archival memory. I look forward to seeing your set design, which is one of your drawings.

WK: Yes. I hope you enjoy the show. I did this piece using a French novel from the 1950s from Cameroon—not from France, but from the francophone Cameroonian colony. It's a kind of dramatized reading of the novel.

BLVR: You must be very excited about it being here in LA.

WK: It's a bit scary, actually. We suddenly had to rearrange our cast because one of our cast members was arrested by immigration at the airport in South Africa.

BLVR: Oh no. They couldn't get out of the country?

WK: He couldn't get out. He's Cameroonian. And it turned out his South African residence papers were not in order.

BLVR: Oh dear. Oh dear.

WK: So now we're working with lawyers to sort him out there, but also here we had to rearrange the cast, so a different cast member is taking over his role.

BLVR: Oh, good. You have an understudy?

WK: Well, not an understudy. It's a person who was already a part of the play who is now stepping into the lead role.

BLVR: Right. Oh my goodness.

WK: "Oh my goodness" is right. In fact, this new actor is the third actor to step into the role of our lead character. Our

*Drawing from* WEIGHING… *and* WANTING *(Soho Listening with Two Fragments). © 1997 by William Kentridge. Charcoal on paper. Courtesy of the collection of Brenda R. Potter and Michael C. Sandler; Drawing for* Johannesburg—Second Greatest City after Paris. *© 1989 by William Kentridge. Charcoal on paper. Courtesy of the collection of Brenda R. Potter and Michael C. Sandler; Drawing for Monument. © 1990 by William Kentridge. Charcoal on paper. Courtesy of the collection of Brenda R. Potter and Michael C. Sandler; Next four images: Drawing for the film Other Faces. © 2011 by William Kentridge. Charcoal and colored pencil on paper. Courtesy of The Broad Art Foundation, Los Angeles; Drawing for* City Deep *(Miner with Hammer and Pick). © 2019 by William Kentridge. Charcoal on paper. Courtesy of the artist and Marian Goodman Gallery, New York;  Drawing for the film Other Faces. © 2011 by William Kentridge. Charcoal and colored pencil on paper. Courtesy of The Broad Art Foundation, Los Angeles; Drawing for* Tide Table *(Soho in Deck Chair). © 2003 by William Kentridge. Charcoal on paper. Courtesy of the collection of Brenda R. Potter and Michael C. Sandler; Drawing for* Tide Table *(Soho in Deck Chair). © 2003 by William Kentridge. Courtesy of the collection of Brenda R. Potter and Michael C. Sandler; Portage. © 2000 by William Kentridge. Chine collé of black Canson paper on printed text from* Le nouveau illustré *(c. 1906) supported on cream Arches paper. Courtesy of the artist; Drawing from* City Deep *(Miner Beside Pit). © 2018 by William Kentridge. Charcoal and red pencil on paper. Courtesy of the artist and Marian Goodman Gallery, New York.*

original lead character died very suddenly about three months ago.

BLVR: What?

WK: It was a heart attack, a man in his early fifties. So that was a big change, but we've had three months with that change.

BLVR: You had some time, but still, that's very sad.

WK: To fill the role with the second lead actor, we also had to pull from the existing cast because we had to find someone who was already in the visa application process, because it was too late to start over.

BLVR: Because otherwise you couldn't get the second lead actor, the actor that was eventually arrested by South African immigration, to the United States?

WK: Exactly, because American visas take eighteen months.

BLVR: I'm so sorry.

### VII. ON SHADOWS

BLVR: Your show is titled *In Praise of Shadows*. In 2012 you gave a lecture at Harvard that was titled "In Praise of Shadows." And of course—and I brought this with me—there is thea cult aesthetics book *In Praise of Shadows* by Jun'ichirō Tanizaki. How do you understand the valences of shadow meaning?

WK: After I'd given my lecture at Harvard, people said, "You know, there's this Japanese book." I had never heard of it.

BLVR: That is a surprise!

WK: I've read it now, but I had not heard of it then.

BLVR: The book became very important in the United States through the schools of architecture at Yale and UCLA in the '80s and '90s. It became a sort of cult read around aesthetics.

WK: Tanizaki's book deals with a very different kind of shadow than the shadow I am dealing with.

BLVR: What kind of shadow is Tanizaki dealing with? What kind of shadow are you dealing with?

WK: Well, in Tanizaki's book, in my memory, he is mainly talking about darkness. Darkness made by shadows. He is talking about the obscuring of light, as opposed to an image which is revealed by light projecting a shadow onto a wall, which implies an area of lightness around the shadow, as in shadow play, where you're actually talking about light with an area that is obscured.

BLVR: The Tanizaki book is about elevating darkness above light.

WK: The two approaches are actually quite different.

BLVR: They are oppositional or transversal.

WK: They're different questions. In Western philosophy shadows are to be avoided. I think Plato and the cave in the *Republic* are the obvious connection, rather than the Tanizaki connection. I re-read Plato after I'd done my first piece with shadows. I thought, This piece I have just made actually reminds me of the Plato. So I re-read the Plato. The first time I read Plato was at university, as one does.

BLVR: It's one of those texts you can return to again and again.

WK: It is, and when you re-read it,

the big arguments come out of the darkness into the light. And as you come into the light, you get greater knowledge. The ultimate good is the light of the sun. The sun is the Platonic ideal.

BLVR: Light over darkness.

WK: In re-reading Plato, the thing that struck me was the necessity of the metaphor. For the metaphor to work, for the allegory to work, the metaphor and the allegory must be incarcerated. They must be prisoners who are chained to a wall, whose heads are in headlocks. They can't turn their expression toward the light. When one comes later to Stalinist Russia, one talks about beating humanity into happiness with an iron fist. The violence is in the belief that you know better than other people, and in forcing that knowledge upon other people, whether they want it or not. Colonialism would also describe itself as bringing light into darkness.

BLVR: The colonial justification is bringing "light" to the "dark continents."

WK: We think the violence of colonialism is an aberration. But if you go back to the Plato, the metaphor and the allegory work only in terms of authoritarian violence. They work only in the shadows. In the shadows I'm making, I'm saying, OK, you have people looking at shadows cast on the wall, and then the people go out into the light. But down in the cave, you have to have the next collection of people carrying the shadows across the wall for the next set of prisoners to proceed. It is unceasing.

BLVR: You depict processions in your work as often as you depict shadows. You also depict shadow processions.

WK: I don't know how far the first world can push in terms of what it needs from the third world, in order for the first world to operate. But one certainly understands that the wealth of Europe is predicated on poverty outside Europe. ✱

# VALLEY OF THE MANY-COLORED GRASSES

## BY RONALD JOHNSON

Ronald Johnson is one of the special poets for whom the subject of his poem becomes the poem. I mean this both specifically and generally—each poem is so entirely formed, so precise in the focus of its vision, that its life on the page feels preordained. His great theme is not so much (or only) the world, but rather poetry itself: poetry as a way of seeing, hearing, being in, and *being of* the ritual surround. In this sense, it's a poetry preoccupied with sight. Also with speech: the origins and material of language, its roots and branches, and where they point. His poems are dowsing rods held to the ground, alive with its hidden vibrations and messages.

Born in Ashland, Kansas, in 1935, Johnson worked as a cook, caterer, baker, author of cookbooks, and bar manager, primarily in San Francisco, where he was also a cofounder of the Rainbow Motorcycle Club—a "band of lusty roistering men, often partying until dawn" (his phrase). As a poet, he traced his lineage through the objectivists and Black Mountain school, and became, over the course of his career, a talented practitioner of erasure poetry (*Radi os*), concrete poetry (*Songs of the Earth*), ecopoetry, and documentary poetry, before such labels were commonly applied. He had birds in his ears. He was egregiously overlooked and ahead of his time.

*Valley of the Many-Colored Grasses*, recently reissued fifty-four years after its initial publication, comprises shades of each of these modes. Even today, the formal range is astonishing, most of all because the volume feels so unified: its range, if that is the word for its cosmological scope, never feels overstretched, but always of a piece with the "tangled actual" that is Johnson's constant interest. The book's first section, "A Line of Poetry, A Row of Trees," lies as deeply rooted in the Kansas sod as the plants in its pages. Its poems are odes, gardens, still lifes, constellations, small histories depicting the humanimal world.

The draft-phase title for Johnson's *Ark*—his opus, on which he toiled for over twenty years—was "Wor(l)ds."

**Publisher:** *The Song Cave* **Page count:** *150* **Price:** *$18.95* **Key quote:** *"What hand will reach out to see the world?"* **Shelve next to:** *Lorine Niedecker, Eleni Sikelianos, Charles Olson, Henry David Thoreau* **Unscientifically calculated reading time:** *The time it takes for a sunflower to germinate*

This says it all: the two are one. Our words don't only name but also make the world as we encounter it. Through subtle echo and syllabic magic, Johnson instills this two-in-one in the reader's soul. "What words // must I corner like / hedge-hogs // to put them on a page?" he asks. Letters are shy and mystical creatures; they flap and burrow, take on new forms, respire, shed horns and skin. His sentences run "clear / as nails // but with all a lichen's curious thrust." Johnson is a master of brief, assonantal lists—botanical, elemental, radiant. Listen to him on apples: "but wild may brindle // as a cow / may rust like / rock."

His eye often revels in the vegetable realm. It also questions—rather than simply taking for granted—what it means to inhabit a landscape in a historical sense: buffalo bones, songs of extinct pigeons, the absence and enduring presence of its Indigenous inhabitants, and Coronado's search for gold all populate these pages, are continuously exhumed and reexamined. Johnson heeded Charles Olson's call to "*dig one thing or place or man* until you / yourself know more abt that than is possible." The dirt piles, rising around him after so much digging, appear in the text in the form of quotation; a majority of Johnson's poems are intercut with other voices (Thoreau's, Emerson's, Sioux lore, and others) or references to startling etymologies and treasures from his research. Johnson is a poet in response. His poems sprout from epigraphs.

In the second section, "The Different Musics," the conversations open further. The title piece, dedicated to poet Robert Duncan, crisscrosses the field of the page in a smoke of word-spirits. The sound is pure spring: "the reiteration of a red-eyed vireo." I've read it more than twenty times, each time differently. There's also a suite of ten "letters" to Whitman, brimming with erotic "cosmic cud": "the circulatory music of all things, omnipresent & in flux."

At long last: the prairie bard extraordinaire is back in print.

—*Sean McCoy*

# LANDSCAPES

**M**en love corners. They have the right of way as they impinge upon women on the sidewalk, at readings, in alleyways, and in the grocery line. All these cornerings are just trailing vapors of the real fear. The things men don't just restrict but take. Plenty of books exist about what to do with the art of bad men, but changing the channel and walking on the other side of the street no longer cut it. Christine Lai's debut novel, *Landscapes*, offers no illusions about or answers to this problem, but it is a fortifying read nonetheless. Instead of delivering a polemic, *Landscapes* probes the archive of feminist art for new answers, by blending diary entries, close-third-person narration, and criticism. The brushstrokes of a certain painting may offer a fresh state of mind. Ephemera are scrutinized, elevated to a level of significance normally reserved for major plot points.

In a near future filled with ecological and political ruin, an archivist named Penelope documents her partner, Aidan's, historic home as they wait for his brother, Julian, to come for a visit. The family house is finally going to be demolished, now that it is beyond repair. As Penelope ponders the dense work of painter J.M.W. Turner, whose work adorns the home, the spectral role of violence against women casts a shadow over her daily chores.

Like her namesake, the wife of Odysseus, Penelope waits. Meanwhile, the prodigal son, Julian, who assaulted her long ago, sightsees on his journey home. He witnesses the desolation of the fields and carefully constructed biodomes in Italy that protect sacred sites like the Pantheon. The poor have scattered to the four corners of the earth, pleading for help at every turn. In response, Penelope and Aidan convert their home into a makeshift refugee shelter to allow those passing through a safe place to rest.

Lai alternates between portraying the structural violence of climate change and the interpersonal violence that Penelope once suffered at the hands of Julian. Reflections on Ana Mendieta, Louise Bourgeois, and Giambologna's *Rape of a Sabine Women* electrify Penelope as she tries to work through her feelings toward Julian. She asks why men's depictions of such violence present women as complicit in or even enjoying their own assault. She is haunted, flickering with rage, curiosity, and pessimism. Rape is not a plot point or a device, but a cold memory suppressing her ability to live in the present. To find embodiment, Penelope must confront the mundane rhythm of life after loss.

Lai presents a gentle way forward in the wake of trauma, one marked not by indifference but by tending to one's body as one would tend to a house. One must sweep the rubble, gather supplies, go on walks, and carefully cultivate the body memory. The reparative process is not linear or finite. Penelope will never forget what was done to her. Forgiveness is neither here nor there; in fact, to consider artwork about sexual violence may mean setting aside the idea of atonement altogether. Instead, Penelope writes an essay—very like the art criticism interspersed through *Landscapes* itself.

When Penelope is not archiving the rubble of a collapsing world, she sits for a portrait. A refugee painter remarks that no one is ever fully knowable, but in the act of trying to capture someone's essence, something ineffable surfaces. Like Annie Dillard in *Holy the Firm*, Penelope is our martyr. She will go up on the cross and take in the nightmare we're hurtling toward: an eco-fascist future with cosmic fangs and expensive food chains. There is no way forward without penance. Soon Penelope will have to leave her archive of personal apocalypse behind and face the world.

As she sits for her portrait, she recalls her assault at the hands of Julian, falling in love with his brother, and the words of Louise Bourgeois: "my memory is moth eaten, full of holes." Perhaps these very holes also allow an escape from the corners we sometimes find ourselves trapped in. The way out may be just as narrow, dark, and strange as the way in, full of the debris of everyday life.

—*Grace Byron*

**Publisher:** *Penguin Random House Canada* **Page count:** *296* **Price:** *$29.95* **Key quote:** *"Time has been slipping through me, like water through a sieve."* **Shelve next to:** *Walter Benjamin, John Berger, Annie Ernaux, Derek Jarman, W. G. Sebald* **Unscientifically calculated reading time:** *Two long mornings in bed under an electric blanket with a mug of peppermint tea*

*Illustration by Pete Gamlen*

A REVIEW OF

# ALL-NIGHT PHARMACY

## BY RUTH MADIEVSKY

Ruth Madievsky's *All-Night Pharmacy* begins in the underbelly of Los Angeles. The unnamed nineteen-year-old narrator and her chaotic sister, Debbie, frequent Salvation, a former Christian bookstore that was converted into a bar in East Hollywood. Like an LA parking lot in the haunting glow of evening, the place turns majestic at night. Its regulars are the Los Angelenos you never hear about: theater actors turned porn performers, an energy healer who stores a jade egg in her vagina to transform sexual trauma into power, fake art buyers. It's a world of witty banter and emotional repression.

*All-Night Pharmacy*'s heroine and Debbie fit right in. Our narrator crawls from precarious situation to precarious situation in the shadow of cruel and otherworldly Debbie. Through the ache of the sisters' fraught relationship, Madievsky deftly details the gaps in logic one has to leap over in order to achieve a warped sense of intimacy in a dysfunctional family. Though Debbie drags her into downing mystery pills with strangers and driving to deserted overlooks with shady men, the narrator is still flooded with a desire to curl up next to her sister at the end of the night. Like many big sisters, Debbie is equal parts ethereal and terrifying. "Spending time with my sister… was like buying acid off a guy you met on the bus," the narrator says. "You never knew if it would end with you, euphoric, tanning topless on a fishing boat headed for Ensenada, or coming to in a gas station bathroom, the insides of your eyes feeling as though they'd been scraped out with spoons. Often, it was both."

*All-Night Pharmacy*'s world feels like a Phoebe Bridgers song—spooky and sexy, stringing pop culture together with the abject, and always swelling with feeling. The novel is populated with mythological women. Debbie disappears without a trace, pushing the narrator into a complex relationship with a pseudo spiritual guide and fellow member of the Jewish diaspora, Sasha. Then there's the unnamed narrator's mother, who has been in and out of institutions and now rarely leaves the house. Her various mental illnesses evade diagnosis. Her mother's mother, the narrator's grandmother, who immigrated in her twenties from Russia, compulsively tells the story of her father's murder at the hands of the government for teaching the Torah in his basement. She doesn't understand her "spoiled" American daughter's paranoia.

Under the surface of these characters' addictions and obsessions, *All-Night Pharmacy* throbs with generational grief. After hearing a story about how one of Sasha's ancestors survived the Kishinev pogrom by eating a raw, regurgitated potato, the narrator smells the potatoes on her hands, no matter how much she washes them. These encounters that collapse the space between personal and collective loss prompt the narrator to ask the question "Was belonging to yourself even possible?"

As the narrator and Sasha grow closer, the book seems to draw a connection between redemption and queerness, then quickly swerves away from it. Instead, desire operates in more complex ways in *All-Night Pharmacy*, blurring the lines between the erotic, the familial, and the political, with love as the center of the Venn diagram between these categories. Sasha takes the protagonist on an international journey—away from drugs and the shadow of her sister, and toward her own sense of self—only to wind up pointed directly at Debbie once more. At the end of the novel, she is given a choice: Can she untether herself from the past without self-destructing? Can she love without losing herself?

Madievsky uses dry humor, finely dialed insights, and lush, imagistic language to articulate the burdens of the past that we carry in our bodies. Her "diasporic drama queens," as Madievsky has called her characters, represent kaleidoscopic responses to individual and collective loss. LA's cityscape is the fractured glass upon which these divas dance, colliding and then separating on its precarious surface.

—*Rosa Boshier González*

> **Publisher:** *Catapult* **Page count:** *304* **Price:** *$27* **Key Quote:** *"Debbie wore her body like she owned it; for me, it was the other way around. She was only five foot two, but that made her more powerful; you could fall asleep spooning her and wake up with a screwdriver pressed to your throat."* **Shelve next to:** *Jean Chen Ho, Raven Leilani, Sharlene Teo* **Unscientifically calculated reading time:** *4 pedicures*

*Illustration by Pete Gamlen*

# CAPTIONING THE ARCHIVES

A Conversation in Photographs and Text

## LESTER SLOAN    AISHA SABATINI SLOAN

"Insightful, inquisitive, and full of vivid photographs, this powerful work is as beautiful as it is galvanizing."
—*Publishers Weekly*

**Lester Sloan** began his photography career as a cameraman for the CBS affiliate in Detroit, then worked as a staff photographer in Los Angeles for *Newsweek* magazine for twenty-five years. His daughter, noted essayist and National Magazine Award-winning writer **Aisha Sabatini Sloan**, covers race and current events, often coupled with analysis of art, film, and pop culture.

In this father-daughter collaboration, Lester opened his archive of street photography, portraits, and news photos, and Aisha interviewed him, creating rich, probing, dialogue-based captions for more than one hundred photographs. Lester's images encompass celebrity portraits, key news events like Pope John Paul's visit to Mexico, Black cultural life in Europe, and, with astonishing emotion, the everyday lives of Black folk in Los Angeles and Detroit.

---

*Also available from*

OF THE DIASPORA
•

*A Woman's Place*
BY MARITA GOLDEN

*with a foreword by Tabitha St. Bernard-Jacobs*

*Tragic Magic*
BY WESLEY BROWN

*with a foreword by Ismail Muhammad*

*Praisesong for the Widow*
BY PAULE MARSHALL

*with a foreword by Palmer Adisa*

# THE PUZZLE OF INCREDIBLY WIDE AND DEEP KNOWLEDGE

IF YOU COMPLETE THIS PUZZLE, YOU ARE A GENERALIST
OF BROAD SKILL AND GREAT RENOWN

*by Ada Nicolle, edited by Benjamin Tausig*

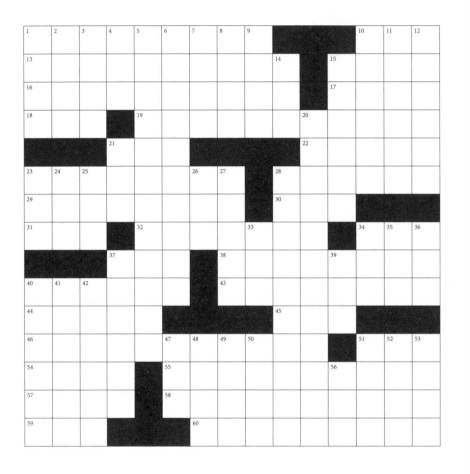

## ACROSS

1. Basic journalistic method, as it were
10. Mac alternative
13. Doing a bit, but only a bit?
15. Primo
16. "That would make zero sense"
17. Establishes
18. Org. surveilling traffic
19. Work that may look really deep?
21. TV cousin referred to as "he," ironically
22. Subject to debate?
23. Second film of Marvel's Phase 4, familiarly
28. Got, ultimately
29. Crush inexperienced competition, in gamerspeak
30. Setting for many early ukiyo-e paintings
31. "Um, actually..."
32. Brand known as Telekom in much of Europe
34. Buying the ___ (investing strategy)
37. ___EO (girlboss, slangily)
38. Their employees work in many fields
40. Unlikely coming-out party honoree
43. Aggressive instruction to a boxer?
44. Going for
45. Behave like a different person?
46. Learned from experience?

51. First professional sports org. to operate an esports league
54. Word before "figures" or "tracks"
55. Fall short of, as a goal
57. It's never covered during news broadcasts
58. Layer of insulation?
59. Tip
60. Start of a correspondence that often reads "I've been good," but not "how about you?"

## DOWN

1. Hard to see the side of?
2. Stewart-___ Racing (NASCAR team)
3. Disney character who sings "Monster"
4. Gender-affirming procedure for some trans people, for short
5. "No clue how the situation ended up this way"
6. Reduced-gravity aircraft, colloquially among pilots
7. Managed, with "by"
8. Collection in a vault
9. Apt rhyme for "blow"
10. Lose time traveling, perhaps
11. Sounding off, maybe?
12. Established by law
14. Rockstar Games series, briefly
15. Requests that one may
20. In fact quite unreliable fact-checking devices
21. Stay in the country, perhaps
23. A high one may be needed to remain fair
24. Ontario 401, e.g.: Abbr.
25. Skywalker nickname
26. Now network, previously
27. They differ for paperback and hardcover editions, for short
28. Star of NBC's "Gimme a Break!"
33. "___ Stay" (2014 film)
34. Gesture performed by Hillary Clinton on an "Ellen" episode
35. Take start?
36. Singer whose first album incurred a fine from the South Korean government
37. Ice formations
39. One trained in AED use
40. Lampoon ___ (Harvard building)
41. Logical statement
42. Word whose last three letters reversed spell something that has its shape
47. Letters in relatable memes
48. Was like
49. Rich source of iron?
50. Opposite of "baja"
51. Element of brilliant writing?
52. Thing sequenced by a sequencer
53. Sooji flour alternative
56. Patti LaBelle's old record label

*(answers on page 118)*

SP /S ⑩ ERRORS HAVE BEEN INERTED INTO THIS PASSAGE. CAN YOU FIND THEM? tr

*by Caitlin Van Dusen*

*PASSING* (1929)
*by* NELLA LARSEN

She felt nauseated, as much at the idea of the glorious body mutilated as fear. How she managed to make the rest of the journey without fainting she never knew.  But at last she was down. Just at the bottom she came on the others surrounded by a little circle of strangers. They were all speaking in whispers, or in the awed, discretely lowered tones adapted to the presence of disaster. In the first instant she wanted to turn and rush back up the way she had come. Then a calm desperation came over her. She braced herself, physically and mentally.

"Here's Irene now," Dave Freeland announced, and told her having only just missed her, they had concluded that she had fainted or something like that, and were on the way to find out about her. Felise, she saw, was holding onto his arm, all the insolent nonchalance gone out of her, and the golden brown of her handsome face changed to a queer mauve colour.

Irene made no indication that she had heard Freeland, but went straight to Brian. His face looked aged and altered, and his lips were purple and trembling. She had a great longing to comfort him, to charm away his suffering and horror. But she was helpless, having so completely lost control of his mind and heart.

She stammered: "Is she—is she—?"

It was Felise who answered. "Instantly, we think."

Irene struggled against the sob of thankfulness that rose in her throat. Choked down, she turned it to a whimper, like a hurt child. Someone lay a hand on her shoulder in a soothing gesture. Brian wrapped his coat about her. She began to cry rackingly, her entire body heaving with convulsive sobs. He made a slight perfunctory attempt to comfort her.

"There, there, Irene. You mustn't." *(answers on page 118)*

*Follow The Chicago Manual of Style, 17th edition. Please ignore unusual spellings, hyphenations, and capitalizations, and the that/which distinction. All are characteristic of the author's style and time.*

# JACKET CAPTCHA
CAN YOU IDENTIFY THESE NINE CLASSIC BOOK JACKETS?

# COMPLETE ME

I started writing when I was _____ years old. I would draw little villages with houses,

schools, churches, cemeteries, and the like, on _____s, and would write stories about

the people living in those villages. I moved around a lot as a kid, but books were a

constant in my life. Some of my favorite childhood book series were _____ _____e on

the _____e and S_____ _____ _____. Over the years, I've had many different kinds

of jobs, and I've worked as an editor at many different magazines, including _____,

which I coedited from 2008 to 2015, and *The Rumpus*, where I was the _____ editor.

My first book, _____, was originally published in 2011 by _____ _____

Press, before being republished by Grove Press in 201_. I am a champion _____

player. In my *New York Times* column, _____ _____, I answer reader questions

about office politics, money, careers, and work-life balance. I also have a newsletter

called ___ _____, and an adorable dog named M_____ _____ _____y.

# CLASSIFIEDS

*Believer Classifieds cost $2 per word. They can be placed by emailing classifieds@thebeliever.net. All submissions subject to editorial approval. No results guaranteed.*

## HELP WANTED

**OMFG PLS HALP ME FIND MY BRAIN**—Did I lose my mind? Yes. Is it a beautiful mind? Okay no, less like Russell Crowe, more like Sylvia Plath (ha!). Is it a poet's mind? Dear god I hope so. Someone tell me I will grow up to write poems. Maybe poems about my brain. If I can find the damn thing. BIANCA. WWW. bianca.fun.

## PUBLICATIONS

**RADIX MEDIA**—is a worker-owned, unionized printer and publisher. Seize the press and build with us. radixmedia.org.

**COST OF PAPER!**—An unprintable publication. costofpaper.com.

**PINE ROW PRESS**—publish your poetry — pinerow.com. *BEAUTIFUL MACHINE WOMAN LANGUAGE* Poems by Catherine Chen, forthcoming Noemi Press, fall 2023.

**WHAT IF POETRY WAS GOOD?** —Forthcoming from Grieveland, a Cleveland-based, volunteer-based indie press in its third year: Matt Mitchell VAMPIRE BURRITO, 6/10; Brendan Joyce PERSONAL PROBLEM, August; Kevin Latimer SOUP, November. grieveland.com.

**WHY IS DORITOS COOL RANCH THE GOD-TIER CHIP?**—Subscribe to LOOSEY at brendonholder.substack.com for bi-weekly essays on culture, technology, humanity, and all the crucial questions. Your group chat will thank you!

## SERVICES

**WHO LET THE DOGS OUT?**—I did, while you were at work, then I re-filled their water bowl and gave them lots of tummy rubs. For all of your Brooklyn-based dog walking and pet caregiving services, including walks, drop-ins, and overnight boardings, contact Emma on Instagram @ewalksbk.

**PENCILHOUSE**—We read WIPs and write feedback on 'em, simple as that. FREE submissions monthly, capacity-capped; $6/mo for submit-whenever, cap-free subs. ALWAYS SEEKING VOLUNTEER CRITICS. pencilhouse.org.

## EVENTS

**THE INTERVAL READING SERIES**—will return to New York City's KGB Bar on August 10th. Readers in fiction, nonfiction, poetry, and translation to include Katrine Jensen, Celeste Marcus, Kat Y. Tang, and more. Doors at 7, readings at 7:30. 85 E 4th St, New York, New York.

## ACTUALLY FREE

**YOUR NEW BEST FRIEND!**— 2 year old female mini schnauzer currently living in Manhattan, seeking a new home anywhere in the contiguous United States. Good with kids, other dogs, and people with allergies. Contact mustreallylovedogs@gmail.com if interested. Serious inquiries only!

## FELICITATIONS

**HIP HIP HOORAY**—to Mary for finally scheduling her hip replacement surgery! Can't wait to go salsa dancing with you once you're all healed up!

**YOU DID IT, DOMMY!**—And we're so proud! Can't wait to spend more time with you this summer and to visit you soon in Colorado <3

**WHAT, LIKE IT'S HARD?**— Congratulations Attorney Nava! We love you so much!

**CONGRATULATIONS**—Dr. Utley on finishing med school and matching into your dream program! Thanks in advance for attending to all of our ear, nose, and throat issues.

**ALL OUR LOVE**—to Clara and Joseph on the birth of their beautiful baby boy! Looking forward to meeting your new bundle of joy!

## MISSED CONNECTIONS

**BEN AFFLECK WAS HERE**— Potentially. Probably. Plausibly. No Contact Magazine is newly open for submissions in short-form Fiction, Non Fiction, Poetry. Just think to yourself: would Ben like this? More at nocontactmag.com.

**RIP TASTY HAND-PULLED NOODLES**—All good things must come to and end, and yet—we will miss you dearly. There's a hole in our hearts, and a void in our stomachs. Get well soon </3

**JENNY DREADFUL**—When an issue of *The Believer* was wrongfully placed at my doorstep last year, I promptly hand-delivered it to the addressee, who lived two floors down from me. We had a lot in common, including a mutual enthusiasm for 19th-century penny dreadfuls! I looked forward to the next issue, which sure enough turned up at my doorstep once more, and gleefully went down two floors again. But it seems that the addressee has moved away since? Jenny: I still have your issue and on the off chance you read this, I would love to return it to you. You know where to find me.

On July 29th and 30th on Governors Island, **THE NEW YORK CITY POETRY FESTIVAL** invites poetry organizations and collectives of all shapes and sizes to bring their unique personalities to the festival grounds, which are ringed with beautiful Victorian houses and tucked beneath the wide, green canopies of century-old trees. Produced by The Poetry Society of New York, The NYC PoFest is an entirely free event that brings poetry to new light in the public eye, unites the largest community of poets in the country, and offers a novel setting for readings. Volunteer with us & find out more: newyorkcitypoetryfestival.com

*Illustrations by Tomi Um*

# INTERNATIONAL BESTSELLER LISTS

*See what the rest of the world is reading in this regular feature, which highlights a rotating cast of countries in each issue.*

COMPILED BY GINGER GREENE, ACCORDING TO 2022 ANNUAL LISTS

## POLAND

1. *Empuzjon* by Olga Tokarczuk. *A young man with tuberculosis seeks respite at a famous sanitorium in Lower Silesia.*

2. *Szkoła latania (Flying School)* by Janusz Christa. *In this installment of the popular comic series Kajko i Kokosz, a pair of Slavic warriors fend off robbers who have learned how to fly.*

3. *Start a Fire: Runda pierwsza (Start a Fire: Round One)* by P. S. Herytiera (Pizgacz). *The first in a series by a young author who initially gained recognition from the novels she posted on Wattpad.*

4. *Wiedźmin: Ostatnie życzenie (The Witcher: The Last Wish)* by Andrzej Sapkowski. *Adapted into a popular video game set in the same universe, this collection of stories from 1993 follows the adventures of Geralt, a mutant assassin.*

5. *Projekt Riese (Project Riese)* by Remigiusz Mróz. *Five tourists visit the Owl Mountains, where Nazi Germany carried out its largest construction project for a still-unknown purpose.*

6. *Skazanie (Condemnation)* by Remigiusz Mróz. *In the fifteenth volume of the popular detective series Chylka, lawyer Joanna Chylka investigates a purported suicide.*

7. *Obrazy z przeszłości (Images from the Past)* by Remigiusz Mróz. *Two decades after a girl disappears, village residents begin to find her belongings in the nearby area.*

8. *Start a Fire: Runda druga (Start a Fire: Round Two)* by P. S. Herytiera. *The second book in the series continues with the story of a teenager from Culver City, who is drawn into chaos by a jaded boy.*

9. *Flaw(less): Opowiedz mi naszą historię (Flaw(less): Tell Me Our Story)* by Marta Łabęcka. *Two lonely teenagers from London learn they have more in common than they thought in this novel popularized on Wattpad.*

10. *Wiedźmin: Miecz przeznaczenia (The Witcher: Sword of Destiny)* by Andrzej Sapkowski. *In the collection that follows The Last Wish, Geralt continues to fight monsters and discern evil in an ethically ambiguous world.*

## BRAZIL

1. *Torto arado (Crooked Plow)* by Itamar Vieira Junior. *On a farm in the hinterlands of Bahia, a pair of sisters live with the enduring legacy of slavery.*

2. *Tudo é rio (Everything Is River)* by Carla Madeira. *Shifting between perspectives, this debut novel tells the story of a marriage complicated by a tragic loss and another woman.*

3. *A vida invisível de Addie Larue (The Invisible Life of Addie Larue)* by V. E. Schwab. *Living a lonely existence after making a bargain with the devil, the immortal Addie meets someone who remembers her after three hundred years.*

4. *Eu e esse meu coração (This Heart of Mine)* by C. C. Hunter. *A teenage girl discovers that her heart transplant was the result of a schoolmate committing suicide, and she begins a relationship with his twin brother.*

5. *O avesso da pele (The Flip Side of Skin)* by Jeferson Tenório. *A young Black man named Pedro mourns his father, who died at the hands of the police.*

6. *Dog and Chainsaw* by Tatsuki Fujimoto. *In the first volume of the manga series Chainsaw Man, Denji and his devil-dog with a chainsaw nose fight demons to stave poverty.*

7. *Uma farsa de amor na Espanha (The Spanish Love Deception)* by Elena Armas. *Desperate to find a date for her sister's wedding, Catalina Martín is stuck with a man who infuriates her.*

8. *Jantar secreto (Secret Dinner)* by Raphael Montes. *A group of friends pay their way through college by hosting secret dinners, where they serve human flesh to rich Cariocas.*

9. *A hora da estrela (The Hour of the Star)* by Clarice Lispector. *An idiosyncratic narrator tells the story of a young woman named Macabéa.*

10. *O amor não é óbvio (Love Isn't Obvious)* by Elayne Baeta. *A high schooler goes on a mission to find out everything about her crush's ex-girlfriend and learns about herself on the way.*

## ITALY

1. *Fabbricante di lacrime (The Tear Maker)* by Erin Doom. *After she's been adopted, seventeen-year-old Nica is haunted by an old fairy tale she heard at the orphanage.*

2. *Il caso Alaska Sanders (The Alaska Sanders Affair)* by Joël Dicker. *A police sergeant receives an unsettling letter that prompts him to reopen a solved case.*

3. *Violeta* by Isabel Allende. *A one-hundred-year-old woman describes the events of her life.*

4. *Rancore (Grudge)* by Gianrico Carofiglio. *Former prosecutor Penelope Spada investigates the death of a university baron in the second book of this crime series.*

5. *Le ossa parlano (The Bones Speak)* by Antonio Manzini. *When the body of a young child is discovered, a pessimistic deputy commissioner grapples with human cruelty.*

6. *Il rosmarino non capisce l'inverno (Rosemary Does Not Understand Winter)* by Matteo Bussola. *A short-story collection about the lives of ordinary women.*

7. *Nel modo in cui cade la neve (The Way the Snow Falls)* by Erin Doom. *A recently orphaned girl from Canada moves to California to live with her godfather and his intriguing son.*

8. *La casa delle luci (The House of Lights)* by Donato Carrisi. *A hypnotist is treating a reclusive young girl when her invisible friend begins to communicate with him.*

9. *Spatriati (Expatriates)* by Mario Desiati. *In this coming-of-age romance, a couple struggles against Puglia's social mores.*

10. *Niente di vero (Nothing True)* by Veronica Raimo. *A comic work of autofiction that deals with the dark trials of family life.*

## SOUTH AFRICA

1. *Storm Tide* by Wilbur Smith with Tom Harper. *A family is divided by the American Revolutionary War in this sweeping novel.*

2. *Titans of War* by Wilbur Smith with Mark Chadbourn. *In ancient Egypt, an enslaved man leads the defense against his kingdom's ruthless enemy.*

3. *The End* by Dudu Busani-Dube. *The sixth book in a popular self-published series titled Hlomu.*

4. *Mad Honey* by Jodi Picoult and Jennifer Finney Boylan. *A mother realizes that her son has many secrets after his girlfriend suddenly turns up dead.*

5. *The Promise* by Damon Galgut. *This Booker Prize–winning novel follows the deterioration of a white South African family on their farm near Pretoria.*

6. *The Milk Tart Murders* by Sally Andrew. *Mystery ensues in the Klein Karoo when a Marilyn Monroe fanatic dies while watching one of her movies.*

7. *Children of Sugarcane* by Joanne Joseph. *A woman moves from rural India to Port Natal in this story about indentured labor under British colonial rule.*

8. *Lessons in Chemistry* by Bonnie Garmus. *A disinclined cooking show host finds herself challenging the status quo of 1960s America.*

9. *The Dark Flood* by Deon Meyer. *Two detectives investigate state corruption, imperiling their careers.*

10. *Die verkeerde vrou (The Wrong Woman)* by Irma Venter. *A crime journalist helps police investigate the disappearance of a famous actress.*

# NOTES ON OUR CONTRIBUTORS

**Benjamin Anastas** is the author of three novels and a memoir. Other work has appeared in *The New Yorker*, *Oxford American*, *Harper's*, and *The Paris Review*.

**Natasha Boas** is a transnational curator, writer, and scholar. Her most recent exhibitions with Zineb Sedira and Baya Mahieddine have helped amplify North African women artists internationally. She is based in San Francisco and Paris.

**Rosa Boshier González** is a writer whose fiction, essays, and art criticism appear in *Guernica, Catapult, Literary Hub, The Los Angeles Review of Books, Artforum, Hyperallergic, The Rumpus, The Guardian, The Washington Post,* and *The New York Times*, among other publications. She serves as the editor in chief of *Gulf Coast* journal.

**Dylan Byron** lives in Paris.

**Grace Byron** is a writer from Indianapolis based in Queens, New York. She used to make films. Her writing has appeared in *The Baffler, The Los Angeles Review of Books*, and *The A.V. Club*, among other outlets. She tweets at @emotrophywife.

**Trina Calderón** is a screenwriter, journalist, and author from Los Angeles. She is devoted to stories with social impact and diverse participants.

**Justin Carder** is one of the hosts of the weirdo graphic design podcast, *40,000,000,000,000 DPI*.

**Ama Codjoe** is the author of *Bluest Nude*, finalist for the NAACP Image Award for Outstanding Poetry and the Paterson Poetry Prize. She is the 2023 poet-in-residence at the Guggenheim Museum and the winner of a 2023 Whiting Award.

**Lucy Corin** is the author of the novel *The Swank Hotel* (Graywolf Press, 2021) and three other books of fiction. She's the recipient of an American Academy in Rome's Rome Prize, a National Endowment for the Arts Literature Fellowship, and a 2023 Guggenheim Fellowship in fiction. She lives in Berkeley, California.

**Amy Fusselman**'s first novel, *The Means*, will be out in paperback in July.

**Joshua Hunt** is a freelance writer for *The New York Times Magazine, Vanity Fair*, and *GQ*.

**Jennifer Kabat**'s twinned books, *Gentian* and *Nightshining*, will be published by Milkweed Editions in 2024 and 2025. Awarded a Warhol Foundation Arts Writers Grant for her criticism, she has written for *Frieze, Granta, BOMB, Harper's,* and *McSweeney's* and been included in *Best American Essays*. An apprentice herbalist, she lives in rural Upstate New York and teaches in the Design Research MA program at SVA.

**Melissa Locker** is a writer and music podcast impresario in the making. She lives on the internet and runs on coffee. You can follow her at @woolyknickers but not in real life.

**Sean McCoy** grew up in Arizona and received his MFA in literary arts from Brown University. He edits *Contra Viento*, a journal for art and literature from rangelands.

**Ted McDermott** is an investigative reporter and the author of *The Minor Outsider*, a novel.

**Jesse Nathan** was raised in rural Kansas and northern California. His first book of poems, *Egglooth*, will be published in September.

**Chris Oliveros** was born in 1966 in Montreal and grew up in the nearby suburb of Chomedey, Laval. He founded the literary comics publisher Drawn & Quarterly in 1989 and was the publisher for the following twenty-five years. Oliveros stepped down from D+Q in 2015 to work on *Are You Willing to Die for the Cause?*, a graphic novel about the early years of the Front de libération du Québec, which hits stores in October 2023.

**Diane Williams**'s eleventh book of fiction, *I Hear You're Rich*, is due out from Soho Press in August. She is the founder and editor of the literary annual *NOON*.

**John Wray** is the author of the novel *Gone to the Wolves*, out now from Farrar, Straus and Giroux.

**Courtney Zoffness** is the author of the critically acclaimed memoir-in-essays *Spilt Milk* (McSweeney's, 2021), named a best debut of the year by *BookPage* and *Refinery29* and a "must-read" by *Publishers Weekly*. She has won the *Sunday Times* Short Story Award and has received fellowships from the Center for Fiction and MacDowell. Her writing has appeared in *The New York Times, The Paris Review Daily, Guernica,* and other venues. She directs the creative writing program at Drew University.

# IN THE NEXT ISSUE

*Not all contents are guaranteed; replacements will be satisfying*

---

# SOLUTIONS TO THIS ISSUE'S GAMES AND PUZZLES

## CROSSWORD

*(Page 112)*

## COPYEDITING THE CLASSICS

*(Page 113)*

She felt nauseated, as much at the idea of the glorious body mutilated as (1) fear. How she managed to make the rest of the journey without fainting she never knew. (2) But at last she was down. Just at the bottom she came on the others (3) surrounded by a little circle of strangers. They were all speaking in whispers, or in the awed, discretely (4) lowered tones adapted to the presence of disaster. In the first instant she wanted to turn and rush back up the way she had come. Then a calm desperation came over her. She braced herself, physically and mentally.

"Here's Irene now," Dave Freeland announced, and told her (5) having only just missed her, they had concluded that she had fainted or something like that, and were on the way to find out about her. Felise, she saw, was holding onto (6) his arm, all the insolent nonchalance gone out of her, and the golden brown of her handsome face changed to a queer mauve colour.

Irene made no indication that she had heard Freeland, but went straight to Brian. His face looked aged and altered, and his lips were purple and trembling. She had a great longing to comfort him, to charm away his suffering and horror. But she was helpless, having so completely lost control of his mind and heart.

She stammered: "Is she—is she—?"

It was Felise who answered. "Instantly, we think." (7)

Irene struggled against the sob of thankfulness that rose in her throat. Choked down, she turned it to (8) a whimper, like a hurt child. (9) Someone lay (10) a hand on her shoulder in a soothing gesture. Brian wrapped his coat about her. She began to cry rackingly, her entire body heaving with convulsive sobs. He made a slight perfunctory attempt to comfort her.

"There, there, Irene. You mustn't."

(1) Insert *from* here for parallel structure: "as much at X as from Y." (2) Delete extra space, a commonly overlooked typo. (3) Insert comma. All the others—not just some of the others—were "surrounded by a little circle of strangers." The lack of a comma suggests that those surrounded by the strangers were a particular subset of "the others," which is not what is meant. (4) *discreetly*. *Discretely*, which means "separately" and *discreetly*, which means "tactfully" or "prudently," are often confused. (5) Insert *that* plus a comma (…told her *that*, having only just missed her, they had concluded…). (6) holding on *to*. *Hold on* is a transitive verb in its own right and is listed as such in *Merriam-Webster's*; the *to* is a separate preposition. (7) Change the straight double quote mark to a closing "smart" (or curly) quote mark. (8) it turned to. This is a dangler: *it*—not *she*—was choked down. (9) child's. The comparison is to a hurt *child's* whimper—not to the hurt child. (10) laid. *Lay* and *lie* are particularly meddlesome verbs, and easily mixed up in their simple past tense and past participle forms; when in doubt, check the dictionary.

---

|   |   |   |
|---|---|---|
| 1 | 2 | 3 |
| 4 | 5 | 6 |
| 7 | 8 | 9 |

## JACKET CAPTCHA

*(Page 114)*

1. *My Brilliant Friend* by Elena Ferrante
2. *Rabbit Redux* by John Updike
3. *The Bell Jar* by Sylvia Plath
4. *Black Leopard, Red Wolf* by Marlon James
5. *The Vanishing Half* by Brit Bennett
6. *2666* by Roberto Bolaño
7. *The Girls* by Emma Cline
8. *Disappearing Earth* by Julia Phillips
9. *Tomorrow and Tomorrow and Tomorrow* by Gabrielle Zevin

## COMPLETE ME

*(Page 115)*

I started writing when I was **four** years old. I would draw little villages with houses, schools, churches, cemeteries, and the like, on **napkins**, and would write stories about the people living in those villages. I moved around a lot as a kid, but books were a constant in my life. Some of my favorite childhood book series were **Little House on the Prairie** and **Sweet Valley High**. Over the years, I've had many different kinds of jobs, and I've worked as an editor at many different magazines, including *PANK*, which I coedited from 2008 to 2015, and *The Rumpus*, where I was the **essays** editor. My first book, *Ayiti*, was originally published in 2011 by **Artistically Declined** Press, before being republished by Grove Press in **2018**. I am a champion **Scrabble** player. In my *New York Times* column, **Work Friend**, I answer reader questions about office politics, money, careers, and work-life balance. I also have a newsletter called **The Audacity**, and an adorable dog named **Maximus Toretto Blueberry**.